TOP DIVE SITES *of the World*

TOP DIVE SITES
of the World

CONSULTANT JACK JACKSON

First published in 1997 by
New Holland (Publishers) Ltd
London • Cape Town • Sydney • Singapore

24 Nutford Place
London W1H 6DQ
United Kingdom

80 McKenzie Street
Cape Town 8001
South Africa

3/2 Aquatic Drive
Frenchs Forest
NSW 2086
Australia

ISBN 1 85368 747 2

SENIOR DESIGNER **TRINITY FRY**
EDITOR **JANE MALIEPAARD**
PUBLISHING MANAGER
MARIËLLE RENSSEN
DTP CARTOGRAPHER
JOHN LOUBSER
ILLUSTRATOR **ANNETTE BUSSE**
PROOFREADER **ANOUSKA GOOD**

Reproduction by
UNIFOTO (PTY) LTD

*Printed and bound
in Singapore by*
TIEN WAH PRESS
(PTE) LTD

ARCTIC OCEAN

EAST SIBERIAN SEA

BARENTS SEA

SEA OF
OKHOTSK

BERING SEA

SWEDEN
FINLAND

NORWAY

ENMARK
ORTH
SEA

Moscow

RUSSIAN FEDERATION

Berlin
GERMANY

POLAND

BELARUS

Paris
ANCE

UKRAINE

HUNGARY

KAZAKHSTAN

MONGOLIA

ROMANIA

ITALY

Rome

Istanbul

Beijing

JAPAN

TURKEY

Seoul

Sardinia

GREECE

Tehran

Tokyo

giers

MEDITERRANEAN
SEA

AFGHANISTAN

CHINA

PACIFIC

ISRAEL

IRAQ

IRAN

LIBYA

Cairo

PAKISTAN

Delhi

TAIWAN

GERIA

EGYPT

Sinai Peninsula

SAUDI
ARABIA

Hong Kong

Port Sudan

INDIA

BURMA

NIGER

CHAD

SUDAN

YEMEN

ARABIAN SEA

BAY OF
BENGAL

Bangkok

Manila

CHINA SEA

PHILIPPINES

Guam

Khartoum

THAILAND

Yap.

Micronesia

Truk

NIGERIA

ETHIOPIA

MALDIVES

SRI
LANKA

Phuket Island

Tubbataha Reefs &
Jessie Beazley Reef

Palau

OCEAN

Lagos

Kuala Lumpur

MALAYSIA

Pulau Sipadan

inea

KENYA

INDIAN

Singapore

Borneo

PAPUA NEW
GUINEA

ZAIRE

Nairobi

INDONESIA

Jakarta

Port Moresby

Solomon Islands

TANZANIA

SEYCHELLES

ARAFURA SEA

Melanesia

ANGOLA

Mozambique Channel

TIMOR
SEA

CORAL SEA

Vanuatu

ZAMBIA

Mauritius
Réunion

Ningaloo Reef

Great Barrier Reef

FIJI

NAMIBIA

ZIMBABWE

MADAGASCAR

OCEAN

AUSTRALIA

Pretoria

Brisbane

Johannesburg

Sodwana Bay

Perth

SOUTH
AFRICA

Durban

Aliwal Shoal &
Protea Banks

GREAT
AUSTRALIAN
BIGHT

Poor
Knights
Islands

Cape Town

Sydney

Dangerous Reef

Melbourne

TASMAN SEA

NEW
ZEALAND

Wellington

ERN OCEAN

The notion of 'world-class diving' is always going to evoke a subjective response. However, images of tropical islands fringed by white sand beaches and turquoise seas, together with exquisite coral gardens on spectacular reefs, seem to hold a universal appeal, attracting divers, underwater photographers, snorkellers, and non-divers alike. Nevertheless, experienced divers also appreciate deep walls on reefs that barely break the surface in open sea; others rave about the bounty found in cold waters. Shallow dives maximize one's

Life on earth began in the ocean, giving marine creatures a head start. The result is one of the world's most complex and diverse ecosystems. Some 200 million years ago, the earth comprised a vast primordial ocean, Panthalassa, surrounding a supercontinent known as Pangaea, which broke up to form the continents we know today.

The Atlantic Ocean formed late in geological time, and was then cut off from the Pacific when the two Americas collided. In the eastern Caribbean Sea, connecting ridges prevent the

TIDES

Tides are caused by the combined effect of centrifugal force and gravitational attraction between the moon and the earth and, to a lesser extent, the sun and the earth. Divers need to understand tides so as to be able to choose the best time to dive according to their preferences. For example, neap tides and slack water are best for taking photographs or for wreck diving. Local tide tables enable divers to calculate flood and ebb tides, and fast or slack water.

descent time, yet some divers favour short, deep 'bounces', hoping to encounter sharks. Many divers prefer leisurely dives, while others seek heart-thumping, shark-feeding frenzies or fierce currents for adrenaline-rush, high-voltage drift dives. Wreck divers often ignore everything else.

In compiling a choice of top dive sites, our criteria included quality, quantity, beauty and uniqueness of marine life; visibility; accessibility; and where available, accompanying attractive sites above water. The selection of destinations offered here celebrates the many wonders of the undersea realm while hopefully appealing to a broad spectrum of active and armchair divers.

Generally, the sites have been grouped together according to the ocean or sea in which they are situated, as these tend to offer particular species and, in some instances, different types of diving. In places, however, the Indian and Pacific oceans are interconnected and have species in common. Sites that fall into these areas have been incorporated into an Indo–Pacific section. Similarly, although the Bahamas are located in the Atlantic Ocean, they have been grouped together with the Caribbean destinations under the Caribbean Sea.

interchange of deep water from the Atlantic, reducing tidal flow. Compared to the Caribbean, the older Indo–Pacific region has 10 times more marine species. During the ice ages, sea levels dropped dramatically, isolating the Red Sea, Gulf of Aden and Arabian Gulf. As a result, 15 per cent of species found here are endemic to these areas.

UNDERWATER VISIBILITY

In mid-oceanic waters, vertical visibility of up to 100m (328ft) is attainable, while in coastal waters it may be affected by rain, river run-off, disturbed bottom sediment, industrial or domestic pollution, landfill, volcanic eruptions, or plankton blooms. By contrast, horizontal visibility greater than 50m (165ft) is usually mythical. In general, visibility is far greater over deep water, or over a rocky or coral bottom. Ebb tides carry sand from beaches and sediment off the top of reefs, reducing overall visibility, while water clarity is usually superior on a flood tide. Local mineral deposits or mining also affect the colour of the water, a phenomenon that is usually only noticed by photographers. With careful buoyancy control, divers can minimize the disturbance of bottom sediment.

SHORE DIVING

Diving from the shore either involves entering the water directly from the shore (preferably a beach), or from a boat that departs for nearby dive sites once or twice a day. Although it is cheaper than live-aboard diving, the accessibility and obvious popularity of most of these dive sites means that they are not as unspoilt or quiet as the more remote offshore reefs; some exceptions are the reefs surrounding Malaysia's Pulau Sipadan and Bonaire and Curaçao in the Dutch Antilles. Other disadvantages to shore diving include a long swim over the reef and having to carry heavy dive and photographic equipment. In sum, shore diving is preferred by those who only wish to dive once or twice a day, or who cannot sleep on a moving boat, or are travelling with non-diving partners.

Above, left to right Crocodilefish (*Papilloculiceps longiceps*) have near-perfect camouflage; a juvenile yellow boxfish (*Ostracion cubicus*); porcupinefish (*Dicotylichthys* spp.) inflate themselves with water when alarmed; the mantis shrimp (*Squilla* sp.) is a fierce predator with mantis-like raptorial claws.

LIVE-ABOARD DIVING

There are several advantages to live-aboard boat diving: it allows more dives per day (between three and five); because the boat sails between sites overnight, diving time is maximized; it has opened up exotic, previously isolated sites, including offshore reefs and wrecks; and there are fewer restrictions on night dives. Live-aboard trips appear expensive, but as you get more dives for your money and all food and accommodation is included, they are good value for serious divers.

Sections of the reef known as walls and drop-offs are usually over deep water, often with very clear visibility. Consequently, it is easy for divers to get too deep without even realizing it. Walls are near-vertical, and may be overhanging or undercut. Drop-offs are slopes of between 60–85 degrees. Divers should never ascend faster than their exhausted air bubbles. In fact, divers are taught to take a five-minute safety stop at 5m (15ft), and a full minute to ascend from this depth to the surface at the end of a dive.

WRECK DIVING

Penetrating large wrecks is an advanced pursuit, and novice divers should only attempt it if they are accompanied by an instructor. Whatever your experience, there are certain obvious precautions that will make your wreck dives safer and more enjoyable. Carry a sharp knife or pair of scissors for cutting fishing line and nets, as well as a good torch, together with a reliable back-up light source; wear tough gloves; and, if possible, plan your dive to coincide with slack water.

REEF DIVING, DROP-OFFS AND WALLS

Reefs may be close to the surface or submerged, and may be sloping or feature a vertical wall, or both. Those with inner lagoons are more suitable for snorkelling; divers prefer to swim over the reef or through a channel for better diving outside. As fringing reefs are inshore and subjected to the effects of land-based activities and processes, they tend to offer poor visibility. They do make fine study areas as they harbour immature species.

Some of the best reefs are submerged in open water washed by tides or currents. Divers may require advanced diving skills and confidence to quickly descend to these reefs and find shelter beside them from the current before they get swept off, but such reefs usually have worthwhile attractions such as sharks and other pelagics.

Above, left to right Trumpetfish (*Aulostomus chinensis*) also exhibit a yellow phase; symbiotic Zooxanthellae produce striking colours in a giant clam's (*Tridacna* sp.) mantle; when disturbed, a Spanish dancer nudibranch (*Hexabranchus* spp.) swims freely; a leafy sea dragon (*Phycodurus eques*).

DRIFT DIVING

Drift diving can vary from pleasantly drifting along a reef in a gentle current, requiring no effort, to high-voltage rushes along walls and gullies, with the possibility of spotting large pelagic species.

Apart from the possibility of physical damage if you hit anything, the main concern when drift diving is becoming separated from your group. Good boat cover is essential, and it is best to use a surface-marker buoy.

NIGHT DIVING

There is nothing to be gained by going too deep on a night dive. An area with minimal wave and current action and easy marks for navigation is best, and the site should first be dived during the day to familiarize yourself with the topography. The easiest night dives are along reef edges, where you can swim out and return along the face.

Before completing the dive, turn off your light for a few minutes. Initially you will be surprised by the crackling noises of the various creatures eating and snapping. As your eyes get used to the dark, you will see many phosphorescent creatures, including flashlightfish and plankton.

Visibility in wrecks is often poor, and it is easy to stir up sediment. If you become disorientated as a result, a lifeline will be your only way of finding your way out again. Leave plenty of air to get out of the wreck and back to the shotline.

CAVE AND CAVERN DIVING

Cave diving requires the same precautions as wreck diving, plus extra precautions not to stir up sediment. Particularly critical is the need to carry extra spares of all important equipment. Divers should always turn back with two-thirds of their air or gas supplies in reserve.

Cavern diving is defined as diving within the line of sight of a cave entrance. The usual safety precautions, torches and a cool head are the only requirements. Changes in currents or exhausted bubbles striking the roof can increase sediment.

QUALIFICATIONS

Divers require a basic certification, or 'C', card unless they are diving on a one-on-one basis with an instructor. This is true for all parts of the world, regardless of depth or currents. Many operators will insist on checking a diver's log book as well.

CARIBBEAN SEA

MEXICO

Yucatán Peninsula and Cozumel Island

CENOTE CAR WASH • CENOTE SAC ACTUN • EL GRANDE CENOTE • PALANCAR REEF

Protruding like a giant thumb from the east coast of Mexico, the Yucatán Peninsula divides the Caribbean Sea from the Gulf of Mexico. Beneath this peninsula lies a world of freshwater-filled cave systems. The entrances to these caverns are known as cenotes, which is a corruption of the Mayan word for 'well'. Today, the Yucatán Peninsula has evolved into a major diving destination for cave and cavern divers from around the world.

Since the early 1980s, over 160km (100 miles) of underground passageways have been surveyed in the Yucatán in and around 80 to 90 cenotes. The most famous cenote of all is Nohoch Nah Chich, which was discovered by Mike Madden in 1987. Some 50km (30 miles) of cave passageways have been explored and charted in this cavern system alone.

Around 50 of the cenotes are found along the Akumal–Tulum Corridor, 100km (62 miles) south of the resort town of Cancún; although well surveyed, they have not yet been completely explored. Cenote diving all takes place on private land, some with crude changing huts or simple platforms at the water's edge.

Mexico's largest Caribbean island, Cozumel, lies just 30km (19 miles) southeast of Cancún on the Yucatán Peninsula. Shaped like a drop jewel, this low-lying island is 47km (29 miles) long and 15km (9 miles) wide. It is covered in large part by dense jungle and swamps, and scattered with the

intriguing ruins of the great Mayan civilization. As well as being rich in history, Cozumel is also blessed with superb beaches lapped by the clear waters of the western Caribbean, and, of course, some of the best diving and snorkelling in the region. A number of hotels, shops and restaurants occur in and around the main town of San Miguel on the west coast of the island. There are some very interesting tours around Cozumel as well as several ancient Mayan ruins to be explored.

Cozumel features a classic example of a petrified, or fossilized, shoreline. The island lies atop a sea mount which was formed by tectonic movements in the earth's crust millions of years ago. This submarine plateau was colonized by coral formations, particularly in the shallow range of the ridge. Vertical coral growth, influenced by rising sea levels, formed perpendicular barriers of coral around the original sea mount. Dropping sea levels, together with wind and wave action, eroded the coral reef until the coastline was typified by a fossilized shoreline surrounded by a live coral fringing reef.

The diving offered along the reefs and shoals of the island's southwest coast is excellent. Virtually all of the diving involves drift diving from a boat and, depending on your skill, dive guides will escort you to the best spot. Besides accompanied boat diving, there are also numerous shore dives at locations along the island's west coast.

CLIMATE Humid, especially from Sep–Jan. Pleasant winters, with average temperatures 20°C (68°F); summer 30–40°C (86–104°F). Eastern trade winds bring rain Apr–May.

BEST TIME TO GO *Cenotes* Nov–Mar (clear water). *Cozumel* Drift diving in very strong currents; calmer clear seas May–Sep.

GETTING THERE *Cozumel* Flights to airport northeast of capital San Miguel, or internal flights from Cancún. Regular ferry services from Puerto Morelos and Playa Del Carman on Yucatán mainland.

WATER TEMPERATURE *Cenotes* Constant 24°C (75°F). Variations occur after rains, and in cenotes connected with sea. *Cozumel* Rarely drops below 27°C (77°F) in winter and 28°C (82°F) during summer.

VISIBILITY *Cenotes* 60m (200ft) in winter; reduced by rainwater. *Cozumel* 30m (100ft) in winter, up to 50m (165ft) in summer.

QUALITY OF DIVES *Cenotes* Cave walls with stalagmites, stalactites and flow stone. *Cozumel* Above-average marine life.

DEPTH OF DIVES *Cenotes* Surface to 12m (40ft). *Cozumel* Surface to 30m (100ft) on wall dives.

SNORKELLING *Cenotes* Possible in some. *Cozumel* Shallower areas along Palancar Reef, as well as all inshore reefs.

DIVE PRACTICALITIES Open-water diving certification not sufficient for cave diving; specialized cave diving certificate essential.

Previous pages The queen angelfish (*Holocanthus ciliaris*) is one of the most colourful Caribbean reef fish.
Opposite The Yucatán Peninsula has an intricate coastline, typified by secluded inlets and fringing reefs.
Top Dive shops, such as this one on Cozumel Island, tout for passing trade with eye-catching graphics.

YUCATÁN PENINSULA

Cenote Car Wash

This remains the most popular cenote, due to its accessibility and very clear water; it is suitable for divers of all levels of skill and experience. Divers are advised to wear a protective suit and hood at all times as this cenote contains tetra and other voracious freshwater fish. They may be small, but they have sharp teeth and can be a real menace. Cenote Car Wash's huge cavern entrance makes it accessible to cavern divers, who by definition have to remain within eyesight of the entrance throughout the dive and do not require any special qualifications. By comparison, cave diving is a more serious undertaking whereby divers move well away from natural sources of light to explore the intricate passages and tunnels of the cave system. A cave diving certificate is essential.

Below The entrance to this cenote is a huge arch which connects to a labyrinth of caves and tunnels.

FORMATION OF CENOTES

More than 250 million years ago, the Yucatán Peninsula was underwater. After millions of years, the sea level dropped to expose a shallow raised plateau of soft porous limestone susceptible to cracking and erosion. Over the centuries, severe tropical rainstorms carved vast underground caverns out of the limestone. A cenote is created when the roof of a cavern collapses, revealing a natural well. Cenotes were a source of fresh water for the Maya, who performed rituals at these sites.

Cenote Sac Actun

With a maximum depth of only 14m (45ft) and a constant temperature of 24°C (75°F), this site never disappoints. Discovered by Steve De Carlo and Jim Coke in November 1988, Cenote Sac Actun features thousands of columns, from straws to chandeliers. People have cried after their first dive in this system, which now has over 5000m (16,400ft) of explored passageways.

El Grande Cenote

El Grande Cenote is a huge collapsed cavern with the centre completely filled in. The entrance to the dive is covered in lily pads. The visibility in the cenote is superb. Gauging visibility is always difficult, but when you are more than 60m (200ft) into a cavern and you can still see someone snorkelling at the entrance, you know that it

Top Water lilies cover the entrance to El Grande Cenote, creating interesting photographs.

is amazingly evident. You dive around the perimeter of the circular hole, from where the cavern system extends well beyond natural daylight to eventually connect into other cenotes where the pattern is repeated, so extending the range. Particularly fascinating are the stalactites, stalagmites, flow stone, and other unusual formations at this site. Spotting another diver in the distance, especially if there are no bubbles surrounding the person, is like watching somebody suspended in midair surrounded by cathedral-sized columns.

COZUMEL ISLAND

Palancar Reef

Palancar is a huge, largely pristine reef stretching over 5km (3 miles). It offers an amazing diversity of marine life and coral formations to suit all tastes and levels of diving expertise. For convenience, it has been split into the four dives most popular with the Cozumel Diving Association, which has over 150 registered dive sites around the island.

Topographically, Palancar Shallows is a very interesting site since it rises to around 5m (16ft) in some places, and in others drops in a mini-wall to 18m (59ft). The reef is cut and divided by many fissures and caves. Black corals, such as *Antipathes pennacea*, are found in the deeper parts, and huge stovepipe sponges stretch out from the reef. There are also brightly coloured yellow tube sponges, associated with juvenile yellowhead wrasse, and a number of fish that often hide in the deep tubes of the sponge at night for protection.

Palancar Horseshoe forms a natural amphitheatre cut into the Palancar Shallows stretch of Palancar Reef. It is always dived separately from the other areas. This dive is better in the deeper section where large gorgonian sea fans stretch out into the current, surrounded by fish, corals and invertebrates.

Palancar Caves, although classified as a deep dive, actually comes to within 6m (20ft) of the surface. The reef slopes outwards and has a deeply convoluted lip. Here the corals seem to take on a life of their own, forming spires, buttresses, caves, gulleys and canyons. Deep fissures run under the coral formations and sand slopes plummet off into the depths. Large sheet corals·jut out from the reef, forming overhangs where squirrelfish and bigeyes seek shelter during the day. Divers should take a torch to pick out the true colours of the fish.

Above The fireworm (*Hermodice carunculata*) is more commonly seen at night. It should not be handled, as its fine hairs can easily penetrate the skin.

Palancar Deep is a deeply incised wall with many varied combinations of coral growth. Shoaling fish such as grunts and snappers are in evidence and if you take your time as you exit the caves on the outer edge of the reef, you may catch a glimpse of a green turtle or a spotted eagle ray.

Below Yellowline arrow crabs (*Stenorhynchus seticornis*) are commonly found amid colourful sponges and corals, and are not afraid of divers.

Below The banded coral shrimp (*Stenopus hispidus*) is essentially a cleaner shrimp. Here, a moray eel (*Gymnothorax* spp.) receives undivided attention.

Below A comical sharpnose pufferfish (*Canthigaster rostrata*) hides from its predators on the reef by sheltering in a pink vase sponge (*Niphates digitalis*).

CAYMAN ISLANDS

Stingrays and Spectacular Wall Diving

STINGRAY CITY • BLOODY BAY WALL

CLIMATE Fine weather year-round. Summer temperatures average 30–40°C (86–104°F), dropping to a low of 20°C (70°F) during short winter season.

BEST TIME TO GO May–Sep, although dive operators boast that you can dive every day of the year here. Always possible to find a lee shore, even during worst weather.

GETTING THERE Cayman Airways and some 10 other air carriers offer numerous flights into Grand Cayman from Miami, other Caribbean islands and US cities, as well as London. Internal flights between Grand Cayman and Little Cayman. Number of flights per week depends on season.

WATER TEMPERATURE Drops slightly to 27°C (80°F) during winter months; in summer, rises to 28°C (82°F).

VISIBILITY Excellent; very rarely influenced by tide and current. Averages over 30m (100ft) year-round.

QUALITY OF MARINE LIFE
Higher than Caribbean average with many species represented. Large schools of fish, turtles, manta rays and, of course, stingrays.

SNORKELLING
Clear sheltered lagoons around much of Cayman Islands' shoreline perfect for snorkelling; suitable for all ages.

DIVE PRACTICALITIES Recommended that some form of insulating suit is worn for protection from the sun and from possible coral cuts and abrasions.

First discovered in 1503 by explorer Christopher Columbus, the Caymans are situated in the central Caribbean, 772km (480 miles) from Miami, or a one-hour flight away, and 282km (175 miles) northwest of Jamaica. It is hardly surprising that the Caymans remained a mystery for so long considering their isolated location in the Caribbean, well away from other islands. Previously a dependency of Jamaica, the Caymans have been a British crown colony since 1962 and are still subject to British laws and customs. The three coral islands, namely Grand Cayman, Cayman Brac and Little Cayman, were formed as a result of tectonic plate upheaval within the earth's crust, and are actually the exposed tips of a massive submarine mountain range.

Today, the islands are a sought-after holiday destination for visitors from all over the world. In addition to the obvious pleasure of being able to scuba dive, snorkel and swim in clear warm water, there are countless other activities on offer, including glass-bottomed boat excursions, parasailing, water-skiing, shopping, banking and just plain relaxing – all in a safe environment where the locals provide a friendly welcome.

What makes the Cayman Islands so special for divers is the deep oceanic trench that comes almost to the shore in several locations, and is responsible for the higher than average clarity of the water. It also provides some of the most spectacular wall diving in the Caribbean with near-vertical drop-offs featuring cave and tunnel formations that beg for exploration. The Caymans' dive operators boast that you can dive every day of the year; because of the size of the islands, it is possible to find a lee shore even during the worst weather where safe descents can be enjoyed. Grand Cayman is home to a legendary dive site known as Stingray City. Together with its counterpart, the Sandbar, another site where stingrays have been habituated by feeding, Stingray City has been featured in *National Geographic* and promoted throughout the world on film, video and in magazines.

Dive operators are particularly safety-conscious; the Cayman Islands Watersports Operators Association (CIWOA) is proud of its record and the fact that the Caymans is one of the safest dive locations in the world. The Department of the Environment, which maintains the Cayman Islands' 18 marine parks and environmental zones, has introduced over 200 permanent mooring buoys. The single-pin moorings are changed every year to allow coral regeneration and to spread the load of diver pollution.

Most of the dive sites are only accessible by boat, which entails a 10-minute trip every day to the chosen site. However, you can also hire equipment from any number of dive centres and shore dive to your heart's content. All of the dive centres offer professional service, excellent value, and instruction to a high standard.

Opposite Light reflects off the sand, fringing reef and deep oceanic trench surrounding Little Cayman.
Top Snorkellers interact with southern stingrays (*Dasyatis americana*) at the Sandbar, a shallow site.

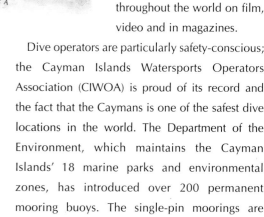

Stingray City

Dubbed 'the world's greatest 4m (12ft) dive', Stingray City is located inside a barrier reef that runs along the north shore of Grand Cayman where the waters are virtually always sheltered and calm. Nothing can prepare you for the first rush of adrenaline when approximately 250 southern stingrays swoop in and envelop you with their 'wings' in their search for a free meal. The accompanying dive guides take frozen squid

ENCOUNTERS WITH STINGRAYS

When diving with stingrays, you are advised to wear a protective suit of some kind to avoid getting a nasty suck from one of these creatures; likened to a love bite, or 'hicky', the mark left by a stingray's suck is not going to be easy to explain to your non-diving partner! Don't ever attempt to ride a stingray or to grab it by the tail. Remember that these are wild animals and if they feel threatened in any way, their defence mechanism is designed to hurt you — as their name implies.

If you do touch one, avoid doing so with gloves, as the fabric can remove the protective mucus layer that covers its leathery skin. If this layer is removed, infection may set in and the stingray may even die as a result.

from a sealed container and feed it to each animal individually. Once the feeding session is over, they become quite docile and can be approached closely. This is the best time to take photographs and to watch them feeding naturally. When they are feeding, stingrays settle on the sea bed and flap their 'wings' in a downward motion to disperse the top layers of sand and expose crustaceans, worms and molluscs.

At Stingray City, the balance between nature and human enterprise is a curious mix, and one is left wondering who is ultimately in command. Suffice to say that several hundred thousand divers have enjoyed memorable interactions with these amazing animals, and will no doubt continue to do so for many years to come.

Bloody Bay Wall

Situated to the north of Little Cayman Island, Bloody Bay Wall is a spectacular site which offers a range of dives, each completely different to the next one. The wall starts at a depth of only 6–8m (20–26ft), which allows you all the time in the

Opposite, left and right Southern stingrays (*Dasyatis americana*) zoom in on the feeding action.

Top, right and far right Molly, an Atlantic manta ray (*Manta birostris*), cruises with her mouth agape, filtering plankton attracted by divers' lights.

world to enjoy its impressive sites. The shallow water is filled with coral canyons and sand chutes which lead you through spectacular caves into the pristine deep blue waters of the outer reef. Although the wall is justifiably famous in its own right, something very special used to happen along a small stretch of Bloody Bay Marine Park during the summer season. Each night at a site known as Eagle Ray Round-up, a fantastic display of underwater acrobatics would take place under the dive boat's mooring buoy. It was the only location known to divers where you could sit on the sea bed in 10m (33ft) of water and train your dive lights on an Atlantic manta ray that swept in and performed barrel rolls (thought to be a courtship display) in front of your eyes. Molly the Manta, as she was known, had a wingspan of over 3m (10ft). Dive torches attracted krill and plankton which she used to scoop up in her cavernous mouth.

Unfortunately, Molly the Manta has not been seen for some time; it is thought that she might have found a mate elsewhere.

Manta rays feed not only at night but also by day, if there is food. When a manta ray feeds, it extends its fleshy mandibles out on either side of its mouth; the mandibles act like the lips of a funnel, concentrating the flow of plankton in towards the mouth. During the day, these fleshy protruberances, which resemble the devil's horns, remain furled for streamlined swimming.

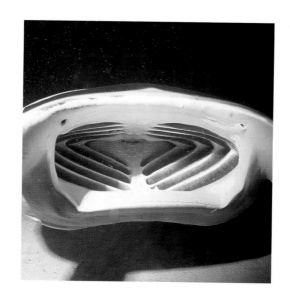

CUBA

The Friendliest Fish in the Caribbean

ISLE OF YOUTH

Shaped like a sleeping crocodile, Cuba lies 145km (90 miles) south of Florida, between Jamaica and the Bahamas. Washed by the Atlantic Ocean to the north, the Caribbean Sea to the south, and the Gulf of Mexico to the west, its 5746km-long (3563-mile) coastline is surrounded by some 4195 cays and islets. In terms of fish life, Cuba is probably the most prolific diving destination in the Caribbean with some 1500 recorded species. It also has some of the longest, cleanest and emptiest white sand beaches in the world.

Both the Atlantic and Caribbean coasts are dotted

with numerous holiday resorts, most of which offer diving as well as facilities for accompanying non-divers. Diving aside, Cuba is rich in unspoilt natural beauty with over 8000 species of flowers, some 300 endemic birds, as well as wild boar and deer. Walking trails traverse the mountain ranges of Pinar del Rio, Escambray, and Sierra Maestra, and near Punta del Este on the Isle of Youth, there are caves decorated with what are thought to be ancient religious frescoes. Some fine examples of Spanish colonial architecture still exist, especially in the capital city, Havana.

Cuba's ultimate diving is off the southwest shore of the Isle of Youth, or the Isla de la Juventud, which is situated 100km (62 miles) south of the southern mainland coast opposite Havana. Previously known as the Isle of Pines, it was the inspiration for Robert Louis Stevenson's classic

tale, *Treasure Island*. Diving centres on the Hotel El Colony, which is situated on the coast west of Siguanea, a 40km (25-mile) drive from Rafael Cabrera Mustelier Airport near Nueva Gerona. The hotel's dive operation is highly organized with 56 marked dive sites and fixed moorings to minimize anchor damage.

The sites are all located between Point Pedernales and Cape Francés, which includes a 6km (4-mile) stretch known as the Pirate Coast. This area has been a marine reserve for more than 20 years and is sheltered from the prevailing winds that blow from the east-southeast; significant currents are also minimal and there are numerous tame and approachable reef fish.

Live-aboard diving is a recent development in Cuba. Cruises to the Archipelago de Los Jardines de la Regina have opened up pristine unexplored sites in an area previously protected from fishing, sport diving and tourism.

For as long as America maintains its embargo on Cuba, it will remain a tantalizingly close yet inaccessible destination for most American divers, excepting those who enter via the Mexican back door. Many Canadians, Mexicans and Europeans, however, have discovered Cuba's excellent diving. The reefs are covered in a proliferation of sponges, gorgonians and coral life, and among the crevices and canyons in shallow water there are plenty of colourful reef fish and crustaceans, although few larger species.

Opposite The Hotel Ancon's dive boat approaches the Playa Ancon jetty to pick up the next batch of divers.
Top Divers exit the sea at Cayo Coco, one of the typical white sand beaches along the Cuban coast.

CLIMATE Semitropical, up to 26°C (80°F) Dec–Mar, rising to 32°C (90°F) Jul–Aug. Humidity and rainfall highest Sep–Oct. Hurricanes rare, but possible, Aug–Nov.

BEST TIME TO GO Feb–May among best months. Wet season is May–Oct. Pirate Coast always protected.

GETTING THERE Direct flights to Havana from Europe, Canada, Mexico and nearby South American gateways; restricted flights do operate from Miami. Charter flights from Europe often fly direct to larger resorts. A 25-minute flight by turbojet connects Havana to Rafael Cabrera Mustelier Airport, Nueva Gerona, on Isle of Youth.

WATER TEMPERATURE Average around 26°C (80°F).

VISIBILITY Generally very clear; 30m (100ft) plus.

QUALITY OF MARINE LIFE Diverse and prolific; fish are tame and approachable.

DEPTH OF DIVES Usually shallow, generally less than 30m (100ft); some sites descend deeper than sports divers should go, so always act responsibly.

SNORKELLING All shore dives a paradise for snorkellers of all standards.

DIVE PRACTICALITIES Diving is mostly relaxed; suitable for all standards of divers, except on deeper dives. All operations offer extensive facilities, diving courses and equipment hire.

Above The stripes on Nassau groupers (*Epinephelus striatus*) change colour in different surroundings.

Left A trumpetfish (*Aulostomus maculatus*) forages for food among the coral formations on the reef.

Above Schoolmaster snappers (*Lutjanus apodus*) drift about in small shoals, often in available shade.

Below Azure vase sponges (*Callyspongia plicifera*) grow solitarily or in groups of two or three.

ISLE OF YOUTH

The dive sites off the Isle of Youth mainly comprise a shallow reef crest with caves, crevices and canyons, and drop-offs into the Gulf of Mexico. Some sites are at 30m (100ft) with valleys descending to between 50–80m (165–262ft). The reefs are forested with gorgonian sea fans,

sea plumes and sea rods, as well as bowl, tube, vase and octopus sponges. Black corals are found at 20–30m (65–100ft), which is considered unusually shallow for this particular species.

Large shoals of tarpon barely condescend to move aside as you swim through them. Barracuda, rainbow runners, red snappers, trumpetfish, as well as schoolmaster snappers, follow divers around. Stingrays are camouflaged on the sand bottom, and spiny lobsters, batwing coral crabs and green moray eels abound.

The myriad friendly fish for which this Caribbean destination is renowned include queen and French angelfish, queen and Sargassum triggerfish, black durgon, ocean surgeonfish, blue tangs, foureye and banded butterflyfish, bluestriped and French grunts, Nassau and marbled groupers, as well as Spanish hogfish, parrotfish,

scrawled filefish, bluehead wrasse, and bigeyes. Blue chromis and shoals of snappers also provide a feast for the eyes.

North-northeast of Cape Francés (named after the legendary French pirate François Leclerc), there are three diveable shipwrecks. Although the area has long been associated with pirates, the wrecks are modern and hold little of historical value. The *Jibacoa River* wreck is home to schools of grunts, red and yellowtail snappers, batfish, angelfish, butterflyfish, tarpon, and barracuda. Various shells, crabs, lobsters and shrimps hide in the wreck, and sponges, gorgonians, tunicates and white finger coral carpet the superstructure. The

Spartan wreck has shoals of small fish, grunts, snappers, wrasse, angelfish, and butterflyfish, as well as sponges, gorgonians, crabs, lobsters, and oysters. The third wreck, the *New Groove*, is surrounded by large shoals of schoolmaster, dog and yellowtail snappers, and smaller shoals of grunts. Trumpetfish hide in the gorgonians, and octopuses hide in the boat's nooks and crannies.

Above The beautiful queen triggerfish (*Balistes vetula*) is usually shy and difficult to approach.

Below Majestic French angelfish (*Pomacanthus paru*) epitomize Cuba's reputation for friendly fish.

Above Scrawled filefish (*Aluterus scriptus*) can alter their patterns and colouring dramatically.

BAHAMAS

Stingray, Dolphin and Shark Encounters

DOLPHIN EXPERIENCE • WHITE SAND RIDGE • SHARK RODEO • SHARK WALL • SHARK ARENA

Widely scattered across some 250,000km² (100,000 sq miles) of the southwest Atlantic Ocean, the Bahamas is usually classified together with the other Caribbean destinations and is the largest concentration of islands in the region. Straddling the Tropic of Cancer, it comprise 700 islands, of which only 40 are inhabited, and over 2000 are sandy cays. The islands stretch for 1200km (745 miles) in a southeasterly direction from a point off Palm Beach in Florida to a point north of the eastern tip of Cuba, and extend to 645km (400 miles) at their widest point.

water, it ensures spectacular visibility. The Bahama Banks plateau, which rises from deep ocean to 6m (20ft) from the surface, seeds a constant supply of nutrients which are preyed on by larger creatures. These animals, in turn, are preyed on by animals further up the food chain. As a result, the Bahama Banks act as a breeding and feeding ground for a prolific variety of marine life; they are a particularly favoured mating ground for bottlenose and spotted dolphins.

Most islands offer shallow reefs from 3m (10ft) to 15m (50ft) and deeper reefs at 30m (100ft). Many have drop-offs going deeper than sports divers may descend to. As the islands cover such a large area, there is great potential for discovering new sites in the Bahamas, particularly by live-aboard.

Eighty per cent of the total population lives in and around the Bahamas' capital city, Nassau, on New Providence Island, and in Freeport on Grand Bahama. Grand Bahama, Paradise Island and Nassau have evolved into extravagant resorts with casinos, duty-free shopping and golf courses. The other inhabited islands are sparsely populated, and consequently offer greater rustic charm. There are some fine examples of colonial architecture throughout the Bahamas.

The Gulf Stream originates in deep waters just to the south of the Bahamas, where it is warmed by the tropical sun and pushed north by the trade winds, carrying marine life from the Caribbean into the Atlantic. Acting as a barrier, the Gulf Stream protects the Bahamas from Florida's rain and river run-off, and together with vast oceanic trenches that allow sediment to settle into deep

Mysterious 'blue holes' are another highlight. These sites, given this name because of their dark blue appearance when seen from above, are created when freshwater caves beneath the sea bed, which are originally carved from soft porous limestone, eventually collapse. Combining both reef and cave diving, some blue holes feature swim-throughs, tunnels, caverns and coral heads. Others are affected by the tides or have haloclines, a phenomenon occurring when fresh water rising from aquifers mixes with sea water.

In addition to world-class reefs, blue holes and wrecks, the Bahamas are famous for encounters with stingrays, dolphins and sharks.

Opposite Whether it's Grand Bahama or New Providence, sunsets in the Bahamas are always spectacular.

Top More than 2000 sand cays are scattered throughout the vast turquoise expanse of the Bahamas.

CLIMATE Mild and tropical; temperatures range from 24°C (75°F) in northern Bahamas during winter months (Dec–May) to an average 28°C (82°F) in summer. Hurricanes rare, but possible Jul–Oct.

BEST TIME TO GO Year-round destination.

GETTING THERE Fly to Freeport (Grand Bahama) or Nassau (New Providence) via Miami. Onward connections to most islands. Also various commercial and charter flights to individual islands from West Palm Beach, Fort Lauderdale and Miami. Cruise ship connections available from Miami and Fort Lauderdale.

WATER TEMPERATURES 24°C (75°F) in the northern Bahamas in winter to 29°C (84°F) throughout archipelago in summer.

VISIBILITY Spectacularly clear; 30–60m (100–200ft) except after bad weather.

QUALITY OF MARINE LIFE Diverse and prolific, often very tame. Large pelagics, especially sharks, may be encountered.

DEPTH OF DIVES Often shallow, generally less than 30m (100ft); drop-offs and walls may descend to depths greater than sport divers should dive, so act responsibly.

SNORKELLING Shallow water over coral reefs provides excellent snorkelling.

DIVE PRACTICALITIES Suitable for all standards of divers. All dive operators offer extensive facilities, diving courses and equipment hire.

Much is said about swimming with dolphins, from reputed healing experiences for the sick to the excitement of being accepted by highly intelligent wild animals in their environment. Two of the most reliable opportunities to interact with dolphins are available off Grand Bahama.

Dolphin Experience

This is a highly successful programme which offers everyone an educational encounter with trained dolphins at the southwest end of Grand Bahama in Sanctuary Bay. Swept by tides, the bay provides natural conditions ideal for dolphins. Dolphin Experience also includes open-water interaction with bottlenose dolphins.

Divers are taken about 1km (half a mile) offshore and settle at 15m (50ft) on the sand bottom while the instructors pilot a small boat towards them with trained dolphins swimming alongside. The dolphins' echolocation sonar pings are heard first before they appear, swimming up to the divers, staring into their masks and seemingly posing for their cameras. Occasionally they are joined by pods of wild dolphins; sometimes, spotted dolphins can be seen swimming in pods with the bottlenose dolphins.

White Sand Ridge

For truly wild dolphin encounters, one of the best locations in the area is along White Sand Ridge, a live-aboard-only destination on the Bahama Banks, northwest of the west end of Grand Bahama. Most photographs and films depicting spotted dolphins in the wild were taken here. For many years, a resident pod of spotted dolphins has been known to gather on the Bahama Banks to

root in the sand for crustaceans and flounders. These dolphins are happy to accept the close company of humans and will even interact with them if they mimic dolphin behaviour. As with manta rays, dolphins prefer snorkellers to divers, possibly because the noise from exhaust bubbles upsets them. Dive operators have perfected the art of locating the dolphins, circling in boats to attract these fun-loving creatures to the bow wave which they enjoy riding. Surprisingly, the dolphins do not swim off when the boats stop so divers may join them in the water. Frolicking with these wonderful animals in their own environment is a highly rewarding experience.

DIVING WITH SHARKS

Shark feeds are high-voltage adrenaline-rush experiences that leave participants with a healthy respect for the grace and power of the ocean's apex predators; they are, however, remarkably safe. Few serious incidents have occurred, with only two minor instances in the Bahamas.

Shark feeding as a spectacle began over two decades ago in the Bahamas. Shark Reef, off the northwest of Long Island (Stella Maris), was the site of the first organized shark feed for a German documentary film. Although there are countless sites, some of the best shark diving is found off the southwest corner of New Providence. Operators

may have different names for dives in the same area. The sharks most commonly involved are Caribbean reef sharks. Regularly fed sharks associate approaching dive boats with food, and circle under the boat before divers enter the water. Shark feeding involves pole spears (long poles ending in a spearhead), chain-mail suits and gloves (for protection from bites). The instructors who do it regularly have considerable experience of the sharks' interaction with divers. The feeds are highly regulated; if the sharks become too excited, food is withheld until they calm down. Clients are kept clear of the bait but remain close enough to the action for full-frame, wide-angle photography.

Shark Rodeo

Situated off Walkers Cay, the northernmost island in the Bahamas, Shark Rodeo is an undisputed hot spot for sharks. Dive boats circle over the site, alerting the sharks to imminent snacks. The divers are escorted to the sand bottom at 11m (36ft) where they settle. A large quantity of bait – a mass

Above Spotted dolphins (*Stenella plagiodon*) are highly gregarious, living in groups of 10 or more.

Left Bottlenose dolphins (*Tursiops truncatus*) are more vocal than spotted dolphins.

of frozen fish – is suspended in the water, attracting over 100 sharks. Caribbean reef, bull, blacktip and nurse sharks are occasionally joined by lemon sharks or hammerheads. Most of the sharks attracted to the feed are females; the larger males tend to remain on the periphery of the action. Once the sharks have settled down, the divers are encouraged to approach closer to the feeding circle. As the sharks have not been handfed, they do not associate the divers with food and show little interest in them.

Shark Wall and Shark Arena

New Providence and Andros islands are divided by a deep oceanic trench known as the Tongue of the Ocean. Along the trench's southwest reef, there is a drop-off called Shark Wall populated by purple tube sponges, sea fans, groupers and Caribbean reef sharks.

Shark Arena, another excellent site situated nearby, is characterized by coral heads on sand. Divers gather in a semicircle around the instructor who feeds bait to the sharks in 15m (50ft) of water. Black groupers, yellowtail snappers and green moray eels complement the shark-feeding action.

Right During a shark feed, the instructor wears a protective chain-mail suit and gloves.

PUERTO RICO

The Caribbean's Best-kept Secret

VIEQUES AND CULEBRA · MONA AND DESECHEO · SOUTH COAST

Puerto Rico, the smallest of the Great Antilles, is 153km (95 miles) long and 58km (36 miles) wide. Bounded by the Atlantic to the north and by the turquoise waters of the Caribbean to the south, the island rises from abyssal ocean depths. Around the coastline and a number of offshore islands the relatively shallow seas teem with marine life. There are easy dives on inshore reefs, advanced dives on deep walls, as well as cave diving.

Puerto Rico's interior is dominated by a mountainous spine, the Cordillera Centrál, which reaches 1338m (4390ft) at its highest peak, Cerro de Punta. A variety of tropical vegetation, from rainforest and mangroves to orchids and ferns, is protected in several reserves, the largest of which is the Caribbean National Forest (El Yunque). At the Rio Camuy Cave Park in the northwest, underground rivers run through one of the largest cave systems in the world.

The capital city of San Juan has developed into the Caribbean's busiest hub for trade and traffic. A stroll through the old quarter encompasses five centuries of Puerto Rican history. Not to be missed is a visit to the recently restored 16th-century fort of El Morro, situated on a promontory 42m (140ft) above the sea. From this vantage point, there are magnificent views over the city and across San Juan Bay to a less ancient landmark, the Bacardi Distillery. The piña colada, a cocktail combining local rum, cream of coconut and strained pineapple juice, was first mixed in Puerto Rico.

Excursions around the island can be done either by tour bus or hired car. Distances should not be underestimated; to drive from the east to the west coast takes about four hours. Outside the cities, comfortable accommodation can be found in small boarding houses known as *paradores*. The prettiest scenery can be seen along the Panoramic Route, which runs east–west across the island through the rugged Cordillera Centrál. A detour to the lighthouse at Cabo Rojo is highly recommended for a breathtaking perspective of the convoluted coastline.

There are over 50 dive sites around the mainland, offering a variety of interesting marine life from nesting turtles and manatees (sea cows) to sand dollars. A conservation project, known as the Sea Grant College Program, strives to preserve the island's marine resources. Besides reef maintenance, the programme also protects whales and sea cows; a research station for this purpose exists on the Isla Magueyes. Situated off the south coast, this tiny island is better known for its Phosphorescent Bay, where phosphorescence glows in the water at night. This phenomenon also occurs at Parguera, and around the islands of Vieques and Culebra.

Ponce, a cultural haven on the south coast filled with architectural treasures, is the gateway to Caja de Muertos. This island has been declared a marine reserve to protect the breeding sites of turtles, and to make both locals and tourists more aware of the underwater environment.

CLIMATE Average daily temperatures 25–29°C (77–84°F). Hurricane season (Aug–Sep) is hotter. Trade winds have moderating effect on climate.

BEST TIME TO GO Year-round. Tradewinds die down Aug–Sep, but it can be very hot (also possibility of hurricanes); water temperatures and visibility slightly raised at this time. European high season Dec–Apr.

GETTING THERE Direct flights from major centres to main Caribbean hub, San Juan.

WATER TEMPERATURE Fairly constant, between 25–27°C (77–81°F) Aug–Oct.

VISIBILITY Offshore islands and reefs offer better visibility, usually 50m (165ft) or more. Best from Mar–Nov. Nutrient-rich estuaries, although murky, attract fish and manatees which require seagrass to feed on.

QUALITY OF MARINE LIFE Typical Caribbean marine species; gorgonians, numerous hard coral species, and along south coast's wall, large fish and barracuda. Deposits of turtle eggs at Caja de Muertos.

DEPTH OF DIVES Fairly shallow; rarely deeper than 15m (50ft) around offshore islands while the south coast drops off sharply from 20m (65ft) to great depths.

SNORKELLING Best around offshore islands, especially Culebra, Palominos, Icacos, Lobos, and Caja de Muertos.

DIVE PRACTICALITIES Equipment hire and tuition available.

Opposite At Cabo Rojo, in the desert-like southwest peninsula, steep cliffs provide a dramatic viewpoint.
Top The island's famous cocktail symbolizes the island's exotic mix of Spanish and American culture.

Although Puerto Rico's north coast is usually pounded by waves from the Atlantic, there are sheltered dive sites where shipwrecks and caves in the lava rock formations can be explored when the sea is calmer. Along the eastern coastline and around its offshore islands, especially Vieques and Culebra, conditions are more favourable to divers of all abilities.

The underwater landscape comprises extensive fringing reefs, rocky outcrops, sand channels, and huge coral heads. The offshore islands themselves have wonderful beaches with fine powdery sand, and diving excursions are often combined with a picnic. Most spectacular of all are the dive sites off the south and west coasts, and in the waters surrounding the islands of Mona, Culebra and Desecheo.

Visibility varies according to the prevailing weather. As a rule, the south and west coasts are less affected by river run-off than the rest of the island as there are fewer big rivers in those parts.

Vieques and Culebra

These offshore islands can be reached eastily via small plane or ferry from the mainland. Vieques, which lies 11km (6 miles) from the east-coast port of Fajardo, offers excellent diving along its west coast. There are extensive plains of staghorn coral, while conchs and barrel sponges abound, along with angelfish, turtles, moray eels and sea horses.

Culebra is itself just 8km (5 miles) long but more than 20 surrounding islets provide a variety of dive sites where healthy coral reefs are colonized with sponges and dense with reef fish. The wreck of a tugboat called the *Wit-Power* lies at a depth that is easily within reach of snorkellers. Also of interest is the dive boat *Crimson Rover*, which sits upright on the sea bed at 16m (52ft). At Amberjack Reef, a cleaning station, large shoals of surgeonfish and barracuda often completely surround divers.

Above The longsnout seahorse (*Hippocampus reidi*) inhabits the reefs along Puerto Rico's north coast.

Right A yellow tube sponge (*Aplysina* spp.) stands out amidst a mixed coral garden patrolled by yellowtail snappers (*Ocyurus chrysurus*).

Mona and Desecheo

To the west of the mainland, the crystal-clear waters round the islands of Mona and Desecheo contain what is widely regarded as some of the most unspoilt marine life in the Caribbean. At Mona, where more than 270 species of fish have been recorded, deep walls, terraces and black coral are among the attractions, while Desecheo's sites include coral-encrusted tunnels and caverns.

The region holds its own special appeal in December and January, when humpback whales and other large marine animals, such as dolphins and turtles, pass through these waters on their annual migration. Dive boats from the west and south coasts offer whale-watching trips.

South Coast

Experienced divers are drawn to Puerto Rico's south coast, where spectacular descents along the reef wall offer enough diving alternatives to last a lifetime. Reached by a one- or two-hour boat ride, the wall stretches parallel to the coast for some 35km (22 miles) from Parguera to Ponce, descending in a series of drops from 18–36m (60–120ft) and then vanishing into unknown depths which are beyond the capabilities of sport divers. Sections of the drop-off feature caves, overhangs, deep ravines and even tunnels. Magnificent coral gardens, huge shoals of reef fish, crabs and moray eels are everywhere. Especially notable sites include Fallen Rock, where a huge boulder teeters at the entrance to a deep trench; wrasse, trumpetfish and triggerfish

swarm over and around the monolith. At Hole in the Wall divers can peer down a channel that cuts through an immense stretch of sheer cliff. The site known as Pinnacles has unusual vertical coral formations, while spots such as Barracuda City and Shark Heaven reveal by their names which species lurk beneath the water.

Top A brown octopus sponge (*Ectyoplasia ferox*), stinging hydroids (*Aglaophenia* sp.) and mixed corals provide a hiding place for small reef fish.

Right Hermit crabs (*Dardanus* spp.) are most vulnerable when moving into a larger shell, having outgrown their old one.

CLIMATE Arid desert-like terrain, daily sunshine. Average temperature 28°C (82°F) but with a cooling breeze.

BEST TIME TO GO *Bonaire* West of Bonaire protected, boasting 365 calm days a year. *Curaçao* Summer and autumn; strong winds produce rough seas at exposed sites for remainder of year (especially Jan–Apr). Area west of Willemstad calm year-round.

GETTING THERE *Bonaire* Direct flights from Amsterdam. Local airlines offer flights between other Caribbean destinations, Miami, Atlanta, and nearby South American gateways among others. *Curaçao* Direct flights from Amsterdam and Portugal. Connecting flights from Miami and Atlanta, and other Caribbean islands; cruise-ship traffic throughout Dutch Antilles is heavy.

WATER TEMPERATURE Average 24°C (75°F) in cool season to 27°C (80°F).

VISIBILITY Very clear, 30m (100ft) plus.

QUALITY OF MARINE LIFE Diverse and prolific, tame and approachable.

DEPTH OF DIVES Often shallow, generally less than 30m (100ft); drop-offs and walls may descend deeper, so act responsibly.

SNORKELLING *Bonaire* All shore-diving sites. *Curaçao* Excellent with snorkelling trails laid out in marine park.

DIVE PRACTICALITIES All dive operators offer extensive facilities, diving courses and equipment hire. Certification required.

DUTCH ANTILLES

Bonaire and Curaçao

KLEIN BONAIRE • CURAÇAO'S WRECKS

Situated 80km (50 miles) north of Venezuela in the southern Caribbean, Bonaire is one of three islands known collectively as the Dutch Antilles. Shaped like a boomerang, Bonaire is 39km (24 miles) long and 5–11km (3–7 miles) wide. Due to the trade winds that blow from the east, almost all diving takes place off the leeward west coast and around the circular 600ha (1480-acre) uninhabited islet of Klein Bonaire, or Little Bonaire, which is located 1km (half a mile) offshore. The islanders are friendly, and actively promote ecotourism. Bird-watching is popular on Bonaire, especially in the Washington–Slagbaai National Park where one of two flamingo sanctuaries on the island is located.

The delightful island of Curaçao is the largest and most populated of the Dutch Antilles; it is 60km (38 miles) long and 11km (7 miles) wide. Situated 55km (35 miles) north of Venezuela, midway between Bonaire and Aruba, its natural beauty is enhanced by the colonial Dutch architecture in Willemstad, the capital. Although oil refining supported the economy until 1985, today the island is a diver's paradise boasting consistently crystal-clear visibility and the largest underwater park in the Caribbean.

Both Bonaire and Curaçao lie atop volcanic undersea mountains. Positioned well outside the hurricane belt, the islands are desert-like with minimal freshwater run-off, and have a pleasant warm and dry climate cooled by trade winds.

It seems as if every resort or hotel on Bonaire is involved in, if not dedicated to, diving. The surrounding waters have been a fully protected marine park since 1971 with fixed mooring buoys to minimize anchor damage. Most shore dives are marked on designated yellow stones, and every operator offers buoyancy control courses free of charge. From time to time, certain sites are 'rested' to allow for their recovery. Most of the 85 dive sites, except those around Klein Bonaire, are either accessible from the shore or are a 15-minute boat ride away; even the most remote sites are less than an hour away. To protect the reefs from overdiving, operators limit boat dives to two per day; you can make up for this with unlimited day and night shore dives. The best diving is in the channel between Bonaire and Klein Bonaire, which drops away to 130m (427ft) and features more steep drop-offs than walls, with plenty of corals, gorgonians, sponges, and fish.

Curaçao lacks the constant leeward sites enjoyed by Bonaire, although some protected coves provide calm seas year-round. Apart from Klein Curaçao, an hour and a half by boat southeast from East Point, most sites can be reached from the shore or via a 20-minute boat ride. Most sites are shallow-water areas inshore of drop-offs beginning at 9–12m (30–40ft). Some feature vertical walls dropping to great depths and many have fixed mooring buoys.

Opposite Dive boats must use the fixed mooring buoys provided to avoid any anchor damage to the reef.
Top Curaçao's breathtaking beaches and exceptionally clear waters ensure its popularity with all divers.

Left A 'cleaner' banded coral shrimp (*Stenopus hispidus*) waves its antennae to attract customers.

Below Shoals of blue tangs (*Acanthurus coeruleus*) foraging on shallow reef tops are a common sight.

squirrelfish laze around, and grunts, schoolmaster and mahogany snappers, stoplight parrotfish, Spanish hogfish, and goatfish dash about. Deeper water harbours black coral. Around the corner, to the northwest, there are other worthwhile sites such as Twixt and Munks Haven and, to the east, a site known as The Forest, which is famous for its extensive forest of black corals. Elkhorn corals, sea fans, other gorgonians and sponges fight for space in the shallow water. The wall starts at 12m (40ft), and is home to scrawled and whitespotted filefish, snappers and porcupine pufferfish. Below 15m (50ft), impressive elephant ear sponges provide a perfect background for wide-angle photography.

CURAÇAO'S WRECKS

Established in 1983, Curaçao Underwater Park stretches along the eastern end of the southwest shore from East Point to the Princess Beach Hotel. Central Curaçao Underwater Park continues from the Princess Beach Hotel to Bullen Bay while Banda Abao Underwater Park runs from the Cap St Mary lighthouse to West Point.

Curaçao is rich in both shipwrecks and reefs. The 61m (200ft) *Superior Producer*, a coastal freighter that accidentally sank in 33m (110ft) of water just outside the harbour in 1977, is the premier wreck in the area. Swept by currents, she sits upright, blanketed with orange cup corals, whip corals, anemones and sponges. The ship's wheelhouse is at a depth of 25m (82ft).

KLEIN BONAIRE

Southwest Corner

Located at the very southwestern tip of Klein Bonaire, and famed for its excellent visibility, Southwest Corner is characterized by fairly moderate currents which sometimes become quite strong. The shallows at this site feature magnificent coral structures and larger than usual staghorn corals while cleaning stations attract tiger and yellowmouth groupers and golden coneys. Shoals of blue tangs surge around, and scrawled and whitespotted filefish, as well as French and queen angelfish, are everywhere. As is typical of Bonaire, the smaller invertebrates and fish are popular macro subjects for photographers; banded coral shrimps, spotted cleaner shrimps and chromis are favourites here.

Covered in large gorgonian sea fans, orange sponges and vase sponges, as well as green and purple tube sponges, the wall drops from 12m (40ft) to sand at 36m (120ft), before shelving out into the depths. Groupers, black durgon and

The *Tugboat* (*Towboat* on some charts) is a popular wreck dive, especially for photographers. She lies in 5.5m (18ft) of water near the eastern side of Caracas Bay. Upright, intact and instantly recognizable, this wreck is Curaçao's unofficial

diving emblem. Just over 8m (25ft) long and small enough to be photographed in its entirety, the boat is sufficiently shallow to be enjoyed by snorkellers as well. The wheelhouse is carpeted with orange cup corals while brain coral and gorgonians cloak the outer hull. The engine room portholes allow for easy penetration by ardent photographers with all their equipment. Parrotfish, moray eels and French angelfish are all resident in the boat. On the seaward side of the wreck, a vertical and sometimes overhanging wall rich in stony corals and orange elephant ear sponges drops from 9m (30ft) to 30m (100ft) before shelving gradually deeper.

At the western end of the island, in the Banda Abao Underwater Park, Mushroom Forest begins as a gently sloping reef with *Tubastrea* cup corals in a submerged cave. Further offshore the site slopes away to 15m (50ft), and features mushroom-shaped stony corals. Feeding stations attract fish, and there are green and chain moray eels, spotted drums and lobsters.

Above Lying in shallow water, the wreck of the *Tugboat* is instantly recognizable. Brain corals cover the hull, while gorgonian sea rods festoon the bow.

Right The wreck of the *Superior Producer*, which sank in 33m (110ft) of water in 1977, is swept by currents and covered in corals and sponges.

ATLANTIC OCEAN

SCOTLAND

Ultimate Cold-water Wreck Diving

SCAPA FLOW

Scotland is world renowned for its 'water of life', and the number of whisky distilleries and variety of flavours to be enjoyed in this country is a whisky connoisseur's dream. Traditional recipes for shortbread may travel the globe, but the country's greatest ambassador of all must be the tartan kilt. Steeped in ancient history and fascinating folklore, Scotland has also become famous among divers for world-class dive sites such as Scapa Flow.

The approximate length of Scotland's jagged coastline, including the indentations created by sea lochs and the many offshore islands, adds up to a total of over 10,500km (6525 miles) – the equivalent of travelling from Scotland to Japan. Although there are numerous diving opportunities in both the Atlantic Ocean and the North Sea, divers in search of the ultimate cold-water wreck diving are inevitably attracted to the wrecks in Scapa Flow.

Situated 25km (16 miles) north of the mainland and covering some 190 km² (73 sq miles), Scapa Flow is sheltered by a circle of islands known as the Orkney Islands. The natural harbour of Scapa Flow, which was a British naval base during both World Wars, has the largest concentration of shipwrecks in the world.

Scapa Flow's chief attraction is the remains of the German High Seas Battle Fleet which was scuttled in 1919. Diving on these ancient warships is both an eerie and spectacular undertaking, but unfortunately many of the wrecks are in very deep water. The German Fleet is unquestionably spectacular, but the ships are deteriorating and caution must be exercised by all divers. Some of the wrecks are war graves and special permission is required from the Royal Navy to dive on these ships.

During hostilities which marked the beginning of World War II, Scapa Flow was reinforced by the use of ships sunk deliberately to block access into the bay by enemy vessels. These block ships are in much shallower water than the German Fleet, allowing divers to maximize their time spent exploring underwater.

At present, three battleships, four light cruisers, five torpedo boats, a World War II destroyer, two submarines, 27 large sections of remains as well as equipment used by salvors, 16 known British wrecks, 32 block ships, and two battleships – the *Vanguard* and *Royal Oak* – have been identified.

A number of boat charter operators with an intimate knowledge of the wrecks are based in Stromness and Kirkwall, and are able to provide all the necessary services. One of the operators also offers 'technical diving' with mixed gas systems. As much of the diving is in depths greater than 35m (115ft), Scapa Flow is only for divers with experience. These waters can be challenging, but most of all the diving is exciting and packed with marine life. These facts, plus the remoteness, considerably heighten the Scapa Flow experience.

CLIMATE Very changeable; average daily temperatures affected by wind chill factor. Summer May–Sep, winter Oct–Apr.

BEST TIME TO GO Year-round, although summer much better as sun almost directly overhead, allowing for greatest penetration of light to deeper wrecks.

GETTING THERE Daily car ferry service from Scrabster on Scottish mainland to Orkney Islands, or regular flights to Kirkwall airport from Edinburgh or Aberdeen.

WATER TEMPERATURE Average 7.5°C (46°F) in Feb, 9°C (48°F) in May, 18°C (65°F) in Aug and 10.5°C (51°F) in Nov.

VISIBILITY More favourable during winter months (Dec–Mar). Entrance to Scapa Flow at Burra Sound averages 12–20m (39–66ft); during summer, visibility on German Fleet reduced to 6–10m (20–33ft).

QUALITY OF WRECKS Block ships in shallow water, making them accessible to divers. German Fleet unquestionably spectacular, but deteriorating; exercise caution.

DEPTH OF DIVES Block ships from surface to 12m (40ft). German battleships 35m (115ft).

SNORKELLING Not recommended due to severity of tidal streams in Scapa Flow.

DIVE PRACTICALITIES Never enter a wreck without suitable training and a safety line. Careful buoyancy control essential too. Cold water and wind chill factor make proper thermal drysuits a requirement.

Previous pages Delicate European jewel anemone (*Corynactis viridis*) colonies deserve their evocative name.
Opposite Near the Churchill Barriers, some of the block ships still protrude above the surface of the water.
Top The permanent causeways that act as barriers, as well as links, between the islands are clearly evident.

Above Queen scallops (*Chlamys opercularis*) swim actively if disturbed by predators such as sea stars.

Left Aptly named dahlia anemones (*Urticina felina*) are an integral part of Scotland's marine fauna.

Scapa Flow

The *Inverlane* is one of the many block ships sunk during World War II to deter enemy ships from entering Scapa Flow. Although situated at the entrance to Burra Sound, the dive itself is actually inside the wreck of the *Inverlane* at a depth of 15m (49ft). The bows of the wreck are completely exposed, and the strange sight of the ship rising out of the water hints at the adventure to come. The dive boat ties up alongside the stricken vessel, and the divers climb onto the wreck with all their kit, assemble and dive through one of the many hatches into the hold. Inside the hull, the water is always clear. The deteriorating ribs and spars are covered in the dwarf species of plumose anemones, which come in three different colour variations. Cushion starfish also grow on the superstructure. Small schools of sand eels take shelter in the largest of the holds, and jellyfish seem to pulsate as they glide by, trailing their stinging tentacles behind.

Towards the bow, a more than friendly seal usually scares everyone when they first encounter it in the gloom. The whole of the stern is blown away revealing a huge expanse of twisted metal. Slack water only lasts 10 minutes at the entrance to Burra Sound, so there are strong tidal currents; it is recommended that divers stay inside the wreckage. Shafts of light play through the open

hatchways and there are several exits, depending on the tide. It is a rather strange feeling to climb inside a wreck wearing all of your diving gear and not to venture outside it for the duration of the dive.

The *Brummer* is certainly one of the most photogenic light cruisers that remain of the German High Seas Battle Fleet which was scuttled by Admiral Ludwig von Reuter in 1919. Designed and built in 1913, the *Brummer* was used to lay mines in the paths of allied shipping. She finally sank on 21 June 1919, and now rests on her starboard side in 37m (121ft) of water. With a sharp bow silhouette which sweeps to the left, the wreck of the *Brummer* is instantly recognizable. As she is deteriorating, divers are advised not to enter the ship. The main superstructure is still intact and the guns are still in position, pointing astern. At the stern, the rudder

now lies on the sea bed. The propeller and its shaft are long gone; being easily accessible, these are always the first parts of a ship to be salvaged.

The superstructure is literally covered in brittle stars, sea squirts, feather stars (particularly *Antedon bifida*), sea urchins and crabs. Large plumose anemones have attached themselves to the outer railings and guns, and the sea bed is littered with shell debris. In sum, this fascinating wreck is one of the best in Scapa Flow. Divers agree that it offers better diving than the massive battleships *Kronprinz Wilhelm*, *Markgraf* and the *König*. Other notable wrecks worth exploring include the *Dresden*, *Köln* and *Karlsruhe*, as well as the *F2*.

Opposite A diver approaches the *Brummer*, which is one of the Flow's most impressive wrecks.

Below, left and right A diver surfaces through a hatchway on the *Inverlane* wreck, leaving behind the eerie, sunlit remains of the ship's interior.

CLIMATE Year-round sunshine with little rain. Northeast tradewinds are stronger Jun–Aug. Average temperature 18–25°C (64–77°F), rising to 30°C (86°F) in summer.

BEST TIME TO GO Sep–Feb for calm water and best visibility; Feb is courting time for rays. High season is over Christmas.

GETTING THERE Flights from all major European airports, as well as charter flights to Tenerife, Fuerteventura, Lanzarote and Gran Canaria. Inter-island transfers via aeroplane or ferry to La Gomera, El Hierro and La Palma also available.

WATER TEMPERATURE 15–25°C (59–77°F).

VISIBILITY Best during Nov–Feb, 10–30m (33–100ft). Northeast tradewinds affect visibility and produce high swell Jun–Aug.

QUALITY OF MARINE LIFE Interesting combination of tropical and cold-water Atlantic species. Rocks overgrown with colourful profusion of sponges, algae and mussels. Pupping ground for sharks and rays. Pilot whales congregate between Tenerife and La Gomera, especially in Jul.

DEPTH OF DIVES 10–50m (33–164ft).

SNORKELLING Possible in calm weather; numerous rocky outcrops at 10m (33ft) offer shoaling fish, anemones and crabs.

DIVE PRACTICALITIES Turbulence and currents to be expected, especially in deep water. Protection against extreme heat and cold advisable.

CANARY ISLANDS

Volcanic Caves and Grottoes

TENERIFE • GRAN CANARIA • LA GOMERA • LA PALMA • LANZAROTE

Although part of Spain, the Canary Islands are situated some 1120km (700 miles) southwest of the Spanish mainland and 100km (60 miles) off the northwest coast of Africa. The archipelago comprises the major islands of La Palma, El Hierro, La Gomera, Tenerife, Gran Canaria, Fuerteventura, and Lanzarote, as well as six much smaller islands.

The Canary Islands were formed millions of years ago as a result of massive volcanic eruptions under the ocean. Despite their common origin, each island in the archipelago has a unique set of physical characteristics. The island of Tenerife is mountainous, with green, fertile valleys and black sand beaches. Spain's highest peak, Mount Teide, is almost at the centre of Tenerife and rises to 3718m (12,200ft) overlooking a huge volcanic crater. Fuerteventura, in contrast, is desert-like with sought-after white sand beaches. Spanish voyagers in the 14th century called the Canaries the 'islands of eternal spring' and for over a century, they fought for control of the territory, subjugating the original inhabitants, the Guanches, in a series of bloody battles. By 1492, the Spanish had conquered all but one of the Canary Islands.

With year-round sunshine virtually guaranteed, the Canaries are perfect for sunbathing, yachting and windsurfing. Besides the wealth of diverse natural beauty, there are also interesting aspects of the local culture to admire, such as traditional dancing and pretty hand-embroidered tablecloths.

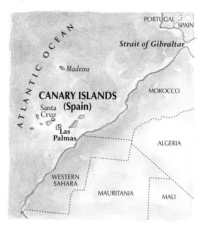

The favourable climate, above-average visibility for at least five months of the year, and relatively close proximity to Europe make the Canary Islands an attractive dive destination, especially for experienced divers in small groups. The volcanic nature of the islands has given rise to fascinating underwater formations. Giant black lava structures alternate with hollowed-out pinnacles, grottoes and arches. Even after millions of years, the rivers of flowing lava that forged this rugged underwater landscape are still visible. In deeper water, between 20–40m (66–131ft), the lava gives way to a glimmering mica sand, forming an interesting contrast to the black rocks. In particular, the island of El Hierro offers exceptional diving in caves and grottoes.

The marine environment in the Canary Islands may come as a surprise to those divers more accustomed to tropical-water conditions. Here, typical cold-water Atlantic species coexist with those of warmer Atlantic waters. Scorpionfish lurk on the sea bed, waiting for their prey, while flatfish and lizardfish can be seen everywhere. Huge shoals of gobies forage in the sand, closely followed by rainbow wrasse and trumpetfish, all hoping to profit. Most sites reveal treasures, especially for divers with an eye for detail. There are many colourful anemones and garden eels, for example, as well as arrow crabs, shrimps and crawfish that often live in close association with one another in secret caves and crevices.

Opposite A beacon on the black rocks of La Gomera's steep coast marks the entrance to San Sebastian harbour.

Top Mount Teide forms a backdrop to the Tenerife resorts of Los Cristianos and Playa de las Americas.

Tenerife

The dive sites to the south of Tenerife are characterized by calm waters, and are suitable for all levels of divers. Diving instruction is available at a number of reputable resorts. The north coast is distinguished by a great diversity of fish species, most notably at sites such as Cathedral and Mountain of the Fish. Other options include diving on the remains of a well-preserved aeroplane wreck, or in caves and grottoes. Longfinned pilot whales visit these waters in summer, with their greatest concentration in July.

Gran Canaria

This volcanic island has a fascinating coastline varying from soaring cliffs to long sandy beaches. At Arinaga on the east coast, there is a marine reserve. There are also numerous cave and grotto dives around Gran Canaria in depths of 8–35m (26–115ft), as well as wreck diving on an old cement freighter where giant rays, barracuda and angel sharks are commonly sighted.

La Gomera

Various dive operations exist on this island, including one at the Tecina Hotel in Playa Santiago, which offers excellent shore-based diving in the nearby bay. Organized dives are also available from San Sebastian from the dive centre on the harbour promenade near the ferry terminal. La Gomera has an extremely varied marine environment. There are several caves as well as interesting lava formations south of San Sebastian. Extensive stands of yellow gorgonian sea fans can be seen in the Valle Gran Rey.

La Palma

If you are looking for deep dives in a rugged environment, characterized by arches and grottoes, then Las Cabras and Malpique Pinnacles are just two of the special sites off La Palma worth diving. Black coral, large grouper and manta rays are commonly spotted in these waters.

Lanzarote

This island is especially attractive to experienced divers. There is a huge variety of fish, large and small, such as tuna, barracuda, groupers, sardines and rays, and sometimes an angel shark can be seen lying on the sand. An abundance of anemones are found on the volcanic rocks and sand, and in the many caves on the reef.

The best dive sites – all accessible from the shore or by boat – are in the vicinity of Puerto del Carmen. Two of them, the Cathedral and the Hole, both between 20–30m (65–100ft), are worth exploring at length. In some locations, you can find red coral and, deeper down, black coral at the sandy bottom of the reef. Also interesting is a site near the old harbour known as the Wrecks. There are eight purpose-sunk wrecks, creating an exciting underwater park for divers.

Left Often found in shallow waters, the striped red lobster (*Enopiometopus antillensis*) is endemic here.

Top The Canaries' rocky, sediment-free landscapes produce excellent visibility, especially in calm water.

MEDITERRANEAN SEA

SARDINIA

Marine Wonders of the Mediterranean

CAPO TESTA TO CAPO FIGARI • TAVOLARA TO CAPO FERRATO • CAPO MARARGUI TO CAPO FALCONE

*L*ying in the middle of the western Mediterranean Sea, Sardinia is Italy's second largest island, approximately 250km (155 miles) long from north to south, and some 100km (62 miles) at its widest point from east to west. With fewer than two million inhabitants, this is one of Italy's least populated regions, and remains largely undeveloped and unspoilt. In the high mountain areas of the interior, there are tracts of very wild, beautiful country.

Sardinia has been subjected to many changing influences throughout its history, from the Carthaginians and Romans to the Pisans and Spanish in later centuries. Evidence of its earlier civilizations exists in numerous prehistoric sites that dot the island, the most striking being the conical stone towers, or *nuraghi*, built by Bronze Age inhabitants. Some 7000 of these structures have been recorded, the largest and best known of which can be seen at Su Nuraxi to the north of Cagliari, the island's capital.

Cagliari, a busy port and industrial centre, is very much a modern city. In its old quarter, which is still encircled by fortifications, a network of lanes leads to the monuments of the city's past. Among these are a massive rock-cut amphitheatre, built by the Romans in the 2nd century, as well as a cathedral, which dates back to the 13th century.

Sardinia has been largely spared the influx of tourists that visit the mainland and has not been engulfed by giant hotel chains. Extensive stretches

of the south coast are remote and can be reached only by boat but, in contrast, some of the northern coastal areas have become the playground for the rich and famous. The Costa Smeralda (Emerald Coast) in the extreme northeast was developed by the Aga Khan and the island as a whole has benefited from the resulting tourist-generated profits. There is much to enjoy in the smaller holiday resorts, many of which still retain the quaint atmosphere of fishing villages. From the quiet northwestern port of Alghero, once a Catalan colony and rich in examples of 16th-century Spanish architecture, a trip can be taken by boat to the marine caves of Neptune's Grotto. Here, visitors can follow a trail on foot through a series of extraordinary subterranean chambers filled with stalagmites and stalactites.

The island has a coastal landscape typified by sandy bays, rocky outcrops and caves, and the fascinating world beneath its emerald-green waters is a well-kept secret among divers in Europe. The full spectrum of Mediterranean species is found here and, although not nearly as flamboyant as that of the tropics, the marine environment can be appreciated and admired for its myriad shapes and colours. Interesting dives can be found almost all round the coast, though many of the prime sites tend to lie towards the north of the island. Divers are taken by inflatable boat from a shore-based centre to the best sites.

CLIMATE Typically sunny Mediterranean weather; average temperatures between 21–29°C (70–84°F).

BEST TIME TO GO Diving season runs May–Oct, late spring best. Avoid holiday crowds Jul–Aug if possible. Most diving centres closed during winter months, so check beforehand if planning a trip.

GETTING THERE Catch a ferry from Italian ports of Genoa, Civitavecchia, Livorno or Naples (booking recommended), or fly to Cagliari, Olbia or Fertilia from all major European cities. On the island, a hired car is highly recommended.

WATER TEMPERATURE In May, increases from a chilly 16°C (60°F) to average between 20–24°C (68–75°F).

VISIBILITY Late spring offers exceptional visibility, between 20–40m (66–130ft). After storms, visibility can be impaired for 2–3 days due to river run-off.

QUALITY OF MARINE LIFE Varied and diverse, including lush plant life and a profusion of fish and invertebrates.

SNORKELLING Along the coastal areas all around the island.

DEPTH OF DIVES Sites which are suitable for sport divers generally between 18–30m (60–100ft). Some dives up to 60m (200ft), therefore requiring decompression training.

DIVE PRACTICALITIES Strong currents are prevalent in the north.

Previous pages To explore Sardinia's sea caves, divers must first complete a specialized cave diving course.
Opposite Sardinia's rugged landscape is characterized by dramatic rock formations such as this sea arch.
Top The deep-blue Mediterranean crashes against the base of sheer cliffs at Punta Maimoni in the west.

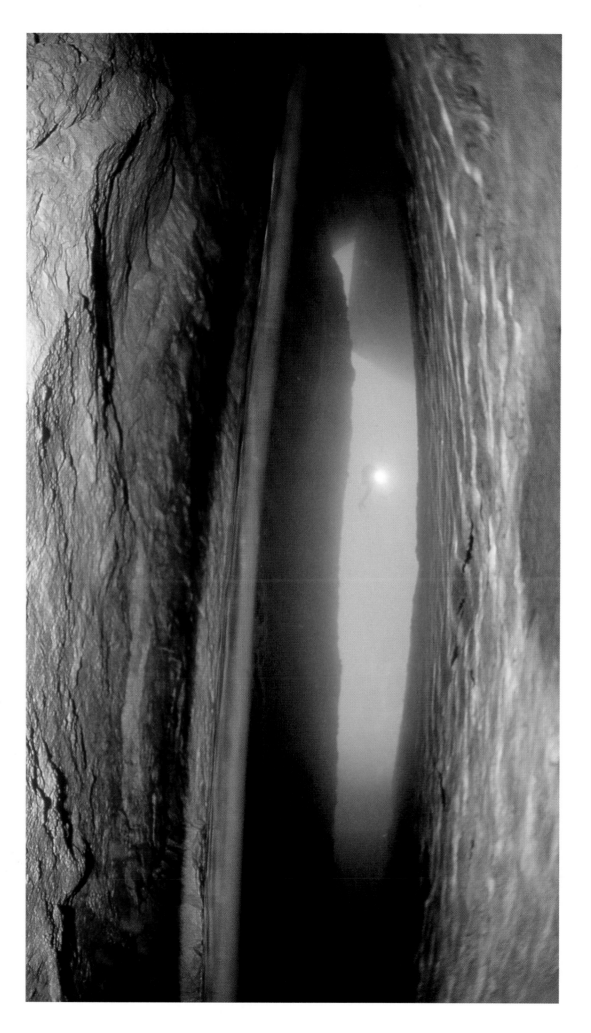

SARDINIA'S MARINE LIFE

Plants, rather than corals, are a feature of diving in Sardinia. In flat bays, where there is sufficient light, extensive meadows of seagrass cover the ocean floor, while in rocky locations, a variety of other algae covers cliffs and boulders. Among the luxuriant growth, snorkellers can observe mussels, cuttlefish and octopus, as well as shrimps, crabs and other invertebrates such as nudibranchs, sea cucumbers, sea urchins and starfish.

Deeper down, there are feather stars, tube anemones and large tubeworms. The rock faces are covered with bryozoans and false corals, and the red barrels of sea squirts can frequently be seen. Cave ceilings are overgrown with anemones and various sponges. In sheltered environments, usually quite deep, there may be true red coral. From 20–30m (65–100ft), gorgonian sea fans of up to 1m (3ft) reach into the current.

Fish life is abundant, and hidden among the fields of algae or in the crevices of the upper regions, you will see blennies, while sea bream and wrasse dance over the seagrass. Damselfish, saupe, combers, and gobies add to the medley, together with sea horses and other pipefish. Divers should beware the venomous dorsal spines of the scorpionfish. Depending on the time of the year, mackerel, tuna and even barracuda find their way from the open sea into these coastal waters. In cracks and caves live Mediterranean moray eels, often together with conger eels.

Capo Testa to Capo Figari

This stretch of Sardinia's far north and northeast coastline offers excellent diving around rock walls and some 30 small islands of the Maddalena archipelago. There are interesting sites featuring underwater cliffs pitted with cavities and in the Secca del Diavolo there is a swim-through wide enough to take several divers. Just beyond Punta Falcone, the wreck of a freighter provides an enjoyable dive. From Capo Figari a number of cave dives are readily accessible. Large sea fans spread everywhere in the currents of the Strait of Bonifacio and black corals are also common.

Left Swimming through spectacular clefts such as this one is the realm of confident divers.

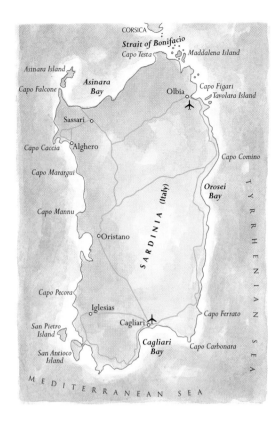

Tavolara Island to Capo Ferrato

Between Tavolara and Molara islands, off the east coast, an underwater granite ridge, the Secche del Fico, rises and falls in a series of peaks and troughs; here, several large groupers may be seen on one dive. Further down the coast there are sandy bays where giltheads and amberjacks congregate in large shoals, particularly during summer. There are also wrecks to explore – even a French aeroplane at 6m (20ft) just north of Capo Comino – and caves inhabited by numerous nudibranchs and lobsters.

Capo Marargui to Capo Falcone

The best-known sites lie to the northwest, with one of the most dramatic being Secca di Capo Marargui. Characterized by canyons, pinnacles and walls, it is frequented by large moray eels. Further north, around Capo Caccia, there are caves and red corals, with sea fans at 36m (120ft). From Capo Falcone, on the far northwestern tip of the island, divers can visit the remains of a Roman shipwreck at Cala del Relitto.

Right Divers' exhausted air, trapped below a cave roof, produces this mirror-like reflection of a diver.

Above A scorpionfish (*Scorpaena porcus*) lies in wait for its prey, displaying its venomous dorsal spines.

Left A diver investigates a spiny lobster (*Panulirus elephas*) that is partly camouflaged by a red sponge.

Above The common octopus (*Octopus vulgaris*) is the most likely member of the genus to be found here.

Opposite Hermit crabs encourage the growth of algae on their adopted shells for camouflage.

RED SEA

ISRAEL

Eilat's Bottlenose Dolphins

DOLPHIN REEF

CLIMATE Eilat warm and dry in winter, average temperature 20°C (70°F). Hot and dry in summer, averaging 35°C (95°F). Annual rainfall usually minimal.

BEST TIME TO GO High summer, Jun–Aug; very hot, but not as hot as central and southern Red Sea.

GETTING THERE Eilat's small airport does not receive international flights. Direct and charter flights to the military airport at Ovda, 40 minutes away by road.

WATER TEMPERATURE Averages 25°C (77°F) in summer, 19°C (66°F) in winter.

VISIBILITY Lower on average than at other Red Sea dive sites, due in part to heavy industrial activity along coast; average at Dolphin Reef is 12m (40ft).

QUALITY OF MARINE LIFE Highlight is swimming with the bottlenose dolphins at Dolphin Reef Complex. Also unusual fish species, including ghost pipefish and ocean sunfish.

DEPTH OF DIVES At Dolphin Reef, the average is 9m (30ft).

SNORKELLING Excellent with dolphins in the enclosure at Dolphin Reef.

DIVE PRACTICALITIES
Both good buoyancy control and restraint are needed to avoid damage to the heavily stressed marine ecosystem at all Eilat sites. Care should be taken not to harass dolphins in any way when diving at Dolphin Reef.

The Red Sea has always been synonymous with mystery and excitement for divers the world over. Once the preserve of bona fide adventurers such as Hans Hass and Jacques Cousteau, the Red Sea has since opened up to tourism from the resorts in the north to the live-aboard cruises of the south.

But diving is not the whole story. The Red Sea is equally fascinating above the surface as it is below the waves. Surrounded by endless sand desert and backed by rugged mountain ranges, it stretches some 1930km (1200 miles) from north to south along a massive geological faultline, which runs from the Jordan valley all the way to Africa's Great Rift Valley. The region is made up of eight nations, each with its own blend of ethnic and religious cultures: Saudi Arabia, Jordan, Egypt, Israel, Sudan, Eritrea, Yemen, and Djibouti all share the sea's coastline.

Israel's Red Sea coastline is a mere 7km (4 miles), sandwiched between Egyptian Sinai and Jordan at the top of the Gulf of Aqaba. Eilat, Israel's southernmost city and port, takes up most of this shoreline. Precious marine resources are shared with commercial and naval ports, leaving few sites open for divers. Nonetheless, Eilat supports a number of top-notch dive centres and thousands of Israeli and foreign divers flock here for courses and recreational diving despite the emergence of newer, more exotic destinations further down the coast. Almost all diving in the

Eilat area is done from the shore, and dive centres generally arrange transport to and from the sites. Due to its long dive history, the dive centres are technically advanced, professionally run operations staffed by highly trained, multilingual dive guides and instructors.

The Eilat coast follows a similar profile throughout; a shallow reef table offering excellent snorkelling leads to a gentle slope, which at 10m (33ft) or more is followed by a steeper sloping section. The impact of decades of unregulated diving, together with the effect of shipping movements and industrial effluent, has taken its toll, and coral growth here is not as luxuriant as it is further south. There are other attractions, however, such as the presence of unusual fish, and a marine reserve which safeguards the fragile reef ecosystem.

Coral growth is a mixture of hard and soft coral species with concentrations of *Dendronephthya*, *Xeniid*, *Acropora*, lettuce and plate corals. The reefs provide a home for jacks, snappers and surgeonfish, while barracuda, parrotfish and wrasse swim among the coral with grouper and sweetlips. Distinct pinnacles and coral heads attract a diverse concentration of other species, including lionfish and triggerfish. Squid, octopus and colouful nudibranchs dot the reef. But the real highlight of diving in Eilat is Dolphin Reef, a unique marine habitat where both divers and snorkellers can interact with dolphins.

Previous pages A diver observes twobar anemonefish (*Amphiprion bicintus*) hiding in their anemone abode.
Opposite Eilat's Coral World Aquarium Complex is surrounded by stark mountains, sand and clear seas.
Top Bottlenose dolphins (*Tursiops truncatus*) ride the pressure wave from a boat's bow in the Red Sea.

Dolphin Reef

This unusual, privately owned site is a 10,000m² (107,000-sq-ft) patch of reef enclosed by coarse net fencing, and provides a stable environment for a number of semi-wild bottlenose dolphins. Entrance is restricted to groups of divers and snorkellers accompanied by a staff member of the Dolphin Reef Complex, while wooden walkways allow nonswimmers a glimpse of the dolphins.

The maximum depth in the enclosure is 15m (49ft), but most of the reef is much shallower. It consists of a sandy patch reef with small mixed

Left, above and opposite Divers can swim freely with bottlenose dolphins (*Tursiops truncatus*) at Dolphin Reef. Resort staff also organize snorkelling sessions for nonswimmers, the blind, and those normally restricted to wheelchairs.

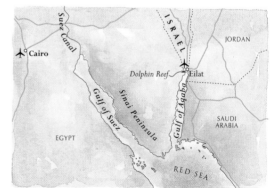

coral heads, as well as a purpose-sunk wreck. Soft coral grows from the boundary fence, exploiting a rich supply of nutrients. Reef fish are common in the enclosure, as are habituated stingrays. The boundary nets exclude any particularly large fish.

Four of the dolphins were born here, and all are accustomed to human contact. Although the gate to the enclosure is opened to let divers in and out, most of the dolphins remain within its boundaries. Some leap over the net to freedom, but almost

always return. This is the only chance most divers will ever have to interact closely with these gentle creatures. It is an exhilarating experience to swim with dolphins, although their fluid grace often leaves clumsy humans bobbing in their wake.

EGYPT

Pristine Corals and a Myriad Fish

RAS MUHAMMAD · BROTHERS ISLANDS · DÆDELUS REEF · *THISTLEGORM* WRECK · ROCKY ISLET

Egypt boasts some of the finest diving in the entire Red Sea, from the coral playgrounds off the southern tip of the Sinai Peninsula through the remote northern coast of the Gulf of Aqaba to the untouched offshore splendours of the deep south which can only be reached by live-aboard boat. Egypt's more than 1500km (950 miles) of desolate coast covers a vast extent of the northwestern Red Sea. There are limitless dive sites from which to choose, including the more remote, pristine locations which are only served by live-aboard boats or land-based safaris.

For the vast majority of foreign divers, Egypt is the Red Sea. The coastal resort towns of Hurghada and Sharm El Sheikh are the region's main dive destinations, and serve as the base for most visitors to the Sinai Peninsula.

High in the mountains, the ancient monastery of St Catherine can be reached in a few hours from Sharm El Sheikh. Here, present-day monks follow spartan monastic traditions that have been in use for some 1500 years. Mount Sinai, 2285m (7497ft) above sea level, is revered by Muslims, Jews and Christians as the place where God delivered the Ten Commandments to Moses. The energetic can follow the 3000 'Steps of Repentance' to the summit; there is also a camel trail to the top. At the coast, stunning reefs and shipwrecks, the legacy of the maritime trade that flowed through the region for millennia, are as steeped in history as they are in natural beauty.

Created in 1983, the Ras Muhammad National Park in the South Sinai region has received the lion's share of international attention over the years. Since much of the country's tourism relies on the Red Sea's fragile reef resources, and considering the volume of diving traffic, it is no surprise that Egypt has emerged as the leader when it comes to marine conservation. As well as numerous shore-based sites from Sharm El Sheikh to the western edge of Ras Muhammad National Park, South Sinai also boasts the Straits of Tiran with their spectacular string of offshore reefs. Away from the coast, this region also contains some of the world's most stunning desert scenery, with rugged, almost lunar mountains forming a stark, beautiful backdrop to the deep-blue waters of the Red Sea.

If you can think of a coral species – or look one up in a reference book – you will almost certainly find a living example in the Egyptian Red Sea. There are branching stony forms like *Acropora* and fire corals, massive porites and favites, delicate flower-like *Dendronephthya* and *Xeniid* soft corals, and gorgonian sea whips and black corals. The fish are as unbelievable as the coral, ranging from hammerhead sharks circling in the blue through huge schools of barracuda to tiny gobies and haloes of anthias that look like Christmas-tree lights. Napoleon wrasse, jacks and surgeonfish in vast schools, as well as manta rays, stingrays, moray eels and crocodilefish all abound.

CLIMATE Summers hot and dry; warm days and cooler evenings during winter. Minimal rainfall. Temperatures fluctuate from below freezing in the desert in winter to 50°C (120°F) in southern Egypt during summer.

BEST TIME TO GO May–Aug. High season Oct–Apr; bookings consequently heavy.

GETTING THERE International airports at Sharm El Sheikh and Hurghada receive direct and connecting flights from all over the world. Resort live-aboard operators arrange local transfers. Most prime sites accessible by live-aboard boat only.

WATER TEMPERATURE Winter lows (Dec–Jan) of 19°C (66°F) to summer highs (Jul–Aug) of 27°C (80°F).

VISIBILITY Averages 20m (66ft) or more year-round; highs of 30m (100ft) common.

QUALITY OF MARINE LIFE Outstanding density and diversity of hard and soft corals and marine life; many pelagics.

DEPTH OF DIVES From 1m (3ft) to well beyond the limits of sport divers. Organized dives usually limited to 30m (100ft).

SNORKELLING Shallow inshore fringing reefs and reef drop-offs easily accessible to snorkellers. Offshore sites also a possibility.

DIVE PRACTICALITIES Some form of protective clothing recommended for fire coral and stinging hydroids. Divers should be self-sufficient and carry all equipment, spares and photographic film.

Opposite Day boats that crowd the famous sites at Ras Muhammad are threatening the survival of the reefs.
Top Ras Muhammad is located at the southern extremity of the Sinai Peninsula where desert and sea meet.

Ras Muhammad

The Ras Muhammad peninsula extends from the Sinai mainland into the Red Sea like a crooked finger. Offshore, there is a dense conglomeration of dive sites within three main areas. The most famous site is Shark Reef, which is the tip of a sheer sea mount rising just off the coast; it is separated from the mainland by a shallow channel. The site boasts a sheer wall dropping to well past 50m (164ft) along its northeast and eastern sides which gives way to a steep reef slope as the reef proceeds southwest. Coral growth is excellent, with dense gardens on the shallower flat areas. Species include *Dendronephthya* and *Acropora*, cabbage and plate corals, and impressive gorgonians. But once you see the fish, you may take no notice of the coral.

Drawn by the big currents that sweep the Ras Muhammad coast, thousands of large pelagics and schooling fish swarm over this reef. Big sharks, among them hammerheads and grey reef sharks, can be seen in the blue, as well as schools of snappers, golden and other trevally, bluespine unicornfish, and fusiliers. The reef is also home to sweetlips, grouper, wrasse and parrotfish.

Brothers Islands

Known locally as El Akhawein, the Brothers are a pair of tiny islands located in open sea off the northern half of the Egyptian coast. The islands are the exposed tips of two massive reef pillars that rise from abyssal depths. These are the only significant reefs for miles in any direction, and they act as a magnet for huge shoals of fish which, in turn, attract sharks. Washed by the full force of open-sea currents, the islands support a diverse coral population with overwhelming growth on all sides. Big Brother lies about 1km (0.6 miles) north of its smaller sibling, Little Brother, easily

identified by a stone lighthouse – a legacy of British rule. A narrow shoreline reef table gives way to a sheer vertical wall, dropping well past the limits of sport diving; fantastic coral growth begins at the surface and continues unabated into the depths. The site favours species that flourish in big currents, such as gorgonian sea whips and a wealth of Red Sea soft corals. The stony corals are also well represented, with innumerable species colonizing the upper wall. Massive congregations of shoaling reef species blanket the wall, and jacks, tuna and barracuda bring their own schools in from the open water to exploit the reef's rich pickings; several shark species are also common.

The soft coral growth at Little Brother is so rich that it looks as if a psychedelic crocheted cap has been popped over the top of the reef. Innumerable surgeonfish, unicornfish and snapper swim by in

Above, bottom and opposite Rich coral reefs rising to within a few metres of the surface are typical of the Egyptian Red Sea. Feeding on plankton, shoals of jewel-bright anthias (*Pseudoanthias* spp.) dart over colourful soft tree corals, stony corals and gorgonian sea fans, retreating to the safety of nooks and crannies in the coral only when predators or divers approach too closely.

Above Masked butterflyfish (*Chaetodon semilarvatus*) are endemic to the Red Sea and Gulf of Aden.

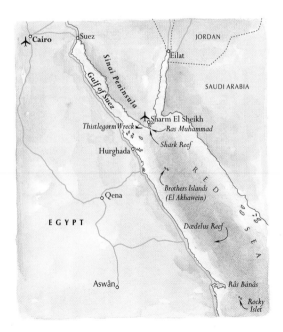

vast shoals. Like at Big Brother, these fish attract sharks, including grey reef, hammerhead, tiger, and even the ominous oceanic whitetip shark. Majestic whale sharks are a tantalizing possibility.

Dædelus Reef

Situated nearly halfway to Saudi Arabia, this small isolated reef known locally as Abu El Kizan is marked by a lighthouse – the only break on the horizon for many miles. Dædelus is famous for sharks, especially thresher sharks, as well as large

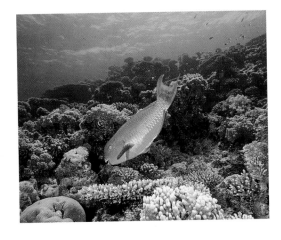

shoals of jacks and a unique shoal of lionfish. The reef drops sheer to 70m (230ft) or more on the east, north and south sides and on the west side, a veritable 'anemone city' boasts an astonishing concentration of beautiful specimens. To the north, the region's best selection of pelagic fish is found – tuna, jacks, barracuda and sharks, along with reef species such as grouper, wrasse, angelfish, triggerfish, and butterflyfish and large concentrations of schooling species such as snappers, unicornfish and surgeonfish.

Below The amazing visibility and strong colours confirm the Red Sea's status as a world-class site.

Above A male steephead parrotfish (*Scarus gibbus*) grazes on algae that grows on coral rock.

Opposite bottom Bright *Dendronephthya hemprichi* soft tree corals are common to the northern reefs.

Above Octopuses can change texture and colour to mimic their surroundings as divers approach.

Above A red sponge (*Cliona vastifica*), black coral (*Antipathes dichotoma*) and sweepers greet a diver.

Above Solitary sabre, or longjawed, squirrelfish (*Sargocentron spiniferum*) feed primarily on crabs.

Thistlegorm **Wreck**

This World War II supply ship sunk by German bombers in 1941 is situated northwest-west of Ras Muhammad in the Straits of Gubal where it is exposed to the prevailing weather. First discovered by Jacques Cousteau, it lies at 30m (100ft) with its largely intact forward section sitting almost upright on the sandy bottom. The centre of the aft section is a jumbled mess, from which you can make out the ship's huge load of artillery shells – this was the epicentre of the blast that sunk the *Thistlegorm*.

Left Divers swim over the coral-encrusted deck of the rediscovered wreck of the *Thistlegorm*.

Above and below World War II BSA motorcycles and other machinery can still be found in the holds.

A railway locomotive that must have been thrown from the deck as the ship sank lies off the port side of the wreck; its tender cars are still on board. The interior of the boat is packed with every possible wartime necessity. The wreck is like a gigantic submerged army surplus store with dozens of BSA motorcycles, car and truck tyres with vehicles to match, and thousands of artillery shells. The site is densely colonized by fish and soft corals, and there are plenty of big jacks, schools of snapper, bannerfish, grouper, and other fish species.

Rocky Islet

Lying 50km (31 miles) off the Egyptian coast and accessible only by live-aboard boat, Rocky Islet (also known locally as Rocky Island) is one of the Red Sea's true gems offering sheer walls and a narrow, sloping sandy shelf exposed to howling currents. A shelf juts from the southeast reef wall at 25m (82ft), forming a natural 'shark theatre' where grey reef, hammerhead, and even oceanic whitetip sharks are often spotted. In addition, there are jacks, snappers, surgeonfish, triggerfish, and barracuda, as well as huge Napoleon wrasse; sweetlips alternate with big parrotfish and colourful angelfish, and smaller damsels, while butterflyfish and brilliant fiery anthias hover over exquisite coral growth.

The reef is ruggedly contoured with many inlets, fissures and cavelets. Coral growth is lush and pristine with soft corals and delicate branching forms making up beautiful inshore shallows. Stony corals are everywhere, and extraordinary sea whips and other gorgonians line the deep walls.

Above A diver passes over coral and sponge growth on the remains of the wreck of the *Thistlegorm*.

Below Twobar anemonefish (*Amphiprion bicintus*), anthias, corals and sponges abound on the wreck.

Above right The shallow wreck of a barge at Bluff Point is commonly used for night dives.

Below right The remains of the *Giannis D 1983*, one of seven wrecks on Sha'b Abu Nuhâs.

SUDAN

Plunging into Diving History

UMBRIA WRECK • SHA'B RUMI • SANGANEB

CLIMATE Inland summer temperatures soar to 47°C (117°F), while coastal temperatures moderated by proximity of sea. Nighttime temperatures often drop below freezing in coastal deserts. Minimal rainfall.

BEST TIME TO GO May–Jul, although conditions in the desert may be extreme. High season Oct–Apr.

GETTING THERE Air connections are notoriously unreliable, particularly to Khartoum; be prepared for delays. Direct flights to Port Sudan from Rome and Cairo recommended, but only available Oct–Apr. Local dive operators smooth the way for you once you land in Port Sudan.

WATER TEMPERATURE Averages 27–28°C (81–82°F); summer highs of 30°C (86°F) produce excellent visibility.

VISIBILITY Year-round average well over 20m (65ft); wall dives often 30m (100ft).

QUALITY OF MARINE LIFE The greatest quantity and diversity of species of all Red Sea species. Pelagics, especially sharks. Excellent soft coral forests and hard corals.

DEPTH OF DIVES Best dives in 15–30m (50–100ft) range. Many walls drop below 100m (330ft), so dive conservatively.

SNORKELLING Offshore reefs, except off points with currents due to sharks.

DIVE PRACTICALITIES No operators or dive shops, so self-sufficiency essential (always carry spares). No instruction offered.

Sudan, the largest country on the entire African continent, lies to the south of Egypt and forms borders with no less than nine other African states, among them Eritrea, Kenya, Ethiopia, and Libya. For all its impressive size, Sudan has a relatively short coastline along the Red Sea – only 650km (404 miles).

Sudan's coast and offshore reefs form a rich, extremely active marine environment. Diving's great pioneers, Hans Hass and Jacques Cousteau, explored these waters for the first time nearly half a century ago and went on to film some of the most enchanting underwater footage the world has ever seen; generations of divers have been inspired by their classic films such as *Le Monde Sans Soleil* (World without Sun), *The Silent World* and *Adventure in the Red Sea*.

Today, the underwater wealth that attracted those early divers continues to draw a select band of diving connoisseurs. Sudan's rickety economy, minimal infrastructure and political unease, however, have combined to make it one of the most difficult Red Sea countries to visit; in fact, the country's southern half is a no-go zone due to the ongoing civil war. Despite this enforced isolation, a few dedicated live-aboard operators and dive companies have continued to keep access to Sudanese dive sites open, and there is a steady trickle of intrepid visitors each year. The complexities of arranging a dive trip to Sudan ensure that divers enjoy virtual isolation on these reefs, which is an added benefit.

Port Sudan is the departure point for all diving in the region. Besides the faded colonial appeal of its wood-balconied houses, there is little of obvious touristic interest on the Port Sudan coast. Most dive operators are based on live-aboard boats, and visitors are usually whisked away from the airport to the harbour. In fact, many divers will pass their entire dive trip without seeing anything of the country. Pre-booked package deals are the only option for diving in Sudan, so you may as well relax and allow the tour organizers to deal with the practicalities of accessing the sites. All live-aboard boats departing from other Red Sea countries must call in at Port Sudan to register and obtain permission to dive in Sudanese waters.

Diving here is enhanced by the thrill of being surrounded by diving history. You can explore the remains of Cousteau's legendary Conshelf II underwater living experiment, follow the route of his maiden voyage aboard *Calypso*, or dive on World War II wrecks such as the *Umbria*.

Sudan's reefs are a riot of colour. Soft coral forests exist side by side with intricate growths of innumerable hard coral species while elsewhere, sheer coral walls carpeted in vivid soft corals plunge to abyssal depths. The reefs are blanketed with fish of every description, from tiny clownfish to bannerfish. Off the reef, barracuda compete for your attention with dolphins and grey reef, nurse, silvertip, silky, tiger and hammerhead sharks, as well as eagle rays and pilot whales.

Opposite Traditional Egyptian cargo boats, known as *sambuks*, are a familiar sight in Port Sudan harbour.
Top A view of the lighthouse and jetty at Sanganeb Reef, the site of many of Hans Hass's early films.

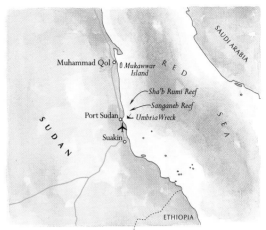

Umbria **Wreck**

In 1949, Hans Hass became the first civilian to dive on this historic wreck. Like the *Thistlegorm* far to the north, the *Umbria* ranks among the finest wreck dives in the world. Lying in the shelter of Wingate Reef and largely unaffected by currents and tides, it is within easy reach of Port Sudan harbour. The ship fell victim to wartime intrigue rather than treacherous seas – she was scuttled by her captain. She lies at an angle on her port side with her starboard davits breaking the surface. At a maximum depth of 36m (118ft), the *Umbria* is shallow by most wreck divers' standards. Snorkellers will be able to explore much of the wreck's upper area while scuba divers will benefit from the extended bottom time possible on the ship's shallower sections. With plenty of light and good visibility, entering most of the ship is easy. The hull itself is completely intact, if heavily encrusted with marine life, and can be explored internally and externally along its entire length.

Left and above Scuttled in a sheltered anchorage in June 1940, the well-lit wreck of the *Umbria* has prolific coral growth and is home to many reef fish.

Sha'b Rumi

If there is a holy grail of Sudanese diving, Sha'b Rumi is probably it. This is the site of Jacques Cousteau's 1963 underwater habitat experiment, Conshelf II, which became familiar to millions of people after his award-winning film *Le Monde Sans Soleil* (World Without Sun). Sha'b Rumi also boasts South Point, a site which is famous for its sharks and numerous shoaling fish.

The site for Conshelf II, which is about 40km (25 miles) northeast of Port Sudan, was chosen for its sheltered windward position, providing safe anchorage for the attendant mother ship, and its proximity to Port Sudan. This location combined a reasonably level ledge at 9m (30ft) for the main station with a drop-off for the deep habitat. Once Jacques Cousteau's experiment had been completed, the two habitats and all the scientific equipment were recovered. Today, the remains (which include the saucer hangar, fish pens and tool shed) provide unlimited scope for divers who want to evoke memories of the early underwater pioneers.

Highlights of the village include the intact onion-shaped dome of the saucer hangar, which is at 9m (26ft). Although the portholes are long gone and the hangar is no longer airtight, the roof does retain the exhaled air of divers; you cannot, however, breath it for long without blacking out! The A-frame equipment shed is pierced by large holes and overgrown with coral. At 30m (100ft) there is a shark cage filled with luxuriant soft coral and shimmering glassfish. The remains of the original 'fish pens' are still on the upper reef, and tend to move around in strong currents.

The remains are all heavily encrusted with hard and soft corals, but little else has changed. Fish are equally abundant, with ample supplies of both reef and pelagic species. Jacks and snappers are seen in big schools, although yacht traffic has affected this.

Sanganeb

Sanganeb, a large atoll 27km (17 miles) northeast of Port Sudan, is the epitome of Red Sea diving with a total of 23 sites. Here, an unbelievably rich tower of pristine coral rises through hundreds of metres of clear blue sea. The huge offshore tower reef is over 8km (5 miles) long and rises from a sea bed over 800m (2624ft) deep. The shallow reef top is packed with vivid corals while sheer vertical walls plunge to immense depths on all sides; to the southwest, a fairly large reef plateau juts into the open sea. This plateau is the centrepoint for Sanganeb dives, and is carpeted in soft corals, hard coral heads and pinnacles. Together with Sha'b Rumi's South Point and the North Point of Sanganeb, many divers regard this as the finest diving in the Red Sea; it is certainly on a par with Papua New Guinea. Sanganeb is also one of the best night dives with Spanish dancer nudibranchs guaranteed directly off the lighthouse jetty.

The entire site is blanketed in reef fish; groupers, wrasse and triggerfish stand out from a very distinguished field, with titan triggerfish swarming in unbelievable numbers. But it is the action offshore that really distinguishes Sanganeb. Silvery pelagics spin round the reef in a shimmering orbit and jacks and tuna abound. They act as a mere appetiser, however, for schools of barracuda that defy belief. Virtually every species of shark in the Red Sea is represented here from blacktip, grey reef and silvertip sharks to huge hammerheads. To round off the day's diving, there is tea and conversation with the keepers of the site's remote lighthouse – the perfect end to one of the Red Sea's most memorable experiences.

Above and left Grey reef sharks (*Carcharhinus amblyrhynchos*) are also known as blacktail sharks (*Carcharhinus wheeleri*) in the northern Red Sea.

Right Notoriously territorial, especially when threatened, grey reef sharks engage in well-defined threat behaviour prior to an attack. Signs include dropped pectoral fins and a stiff body.

INDIAN OCEAN

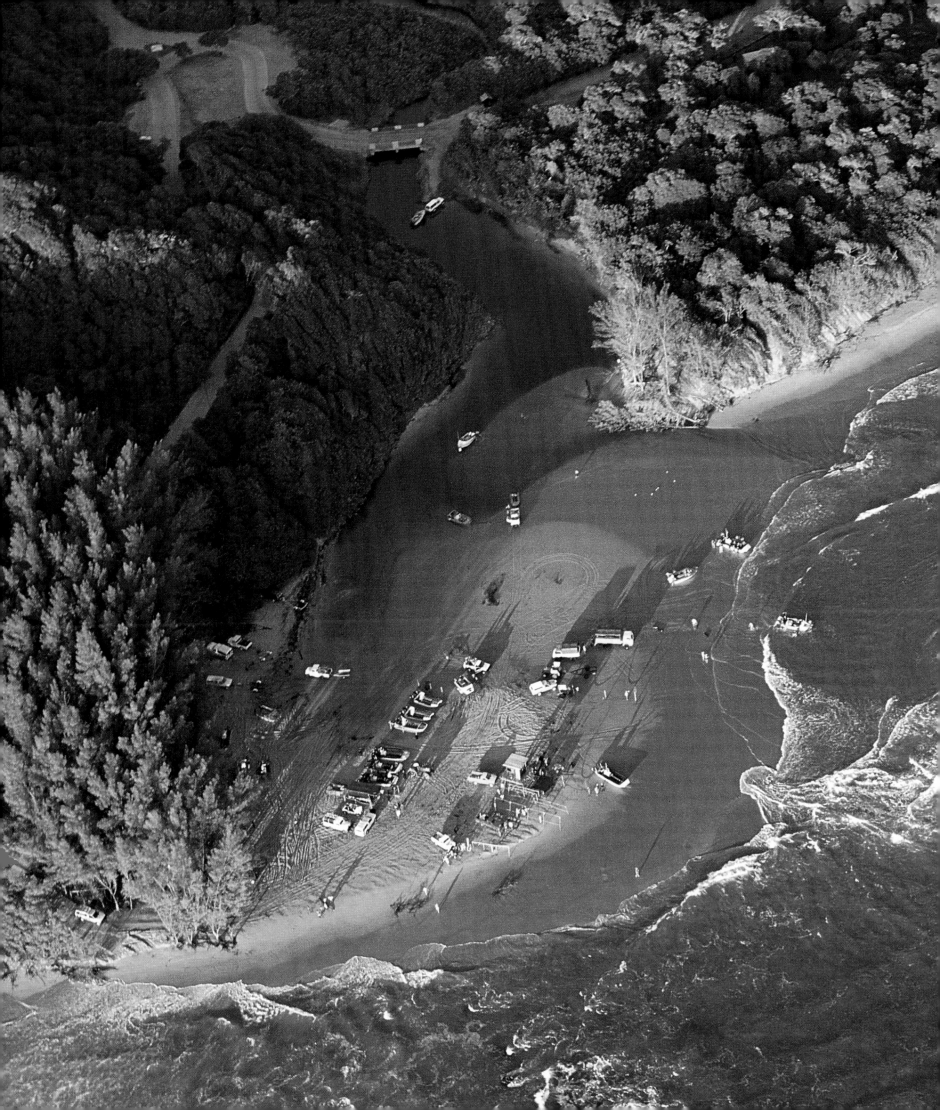

SOUTH AFRICA

Sharks, Game Fish and Nesting Turtles

SODWANA BAY • ALIWAL SHOAL • PROTEA BANKS

Sharks, dolphins, turtles and a rich diversity of marine life are just some of the attractions of South Africa's top dive sites. Sodwana Bay, located 370km (230 miles) north of Durban on South Africa's northeast coast, is home to some of the world's most southerly coral reefs. Underlying Sodwana's reef system is a fossilized dune and beach deposit, which is covered in a 0.5m (1.6ft) layer of coral running parallel to the shoreline. Languishing in the warm water of the Agulhas Current, which flows along the east coast of Africa, these reefs are a perfect breeding ground for a variety of marine creatures; coral heads and overhangs abound with juvenile fish in various stages of development. In addition, Mabibi Lagoon, only 30km (19 miles) up the coast from Sodwana, is a turtle nesting site for green, loggerhead and leatherback turtles.

After Sodwana Bay, Aliwal Shoal, which is 50km (31 miles) south of Durban, is the country's most popular dive site. The Shoal is famous for its raggedtooth (or grey nurse) sharks, which can be seen between August and November. On an average dive, you may see up to 10 sharks. Hammerhead, blacktip, tiger and Zambezi (or bull) sharks are very rare. Several species of ray are common while divers can also look forward to encounters with playful bottlenose dolphins. The area is, however, prone to sudden rises of wind and changes of current so there is no anchoring of dive boats and divers must be equipped with surface marker buoys to indicate their position. Due to the often rough conditions, it is not surprising that a number of wrecks are also dotted about the area. The *Nebo* is now a refuge for many species of fish, while some astonishingly large moray eels await visitors to the *Produce*. Sadly, because of effluent from a nearby paper factory, the future of the Shoal may be threatened.

For experienced divers, Protea Banks on the South Coast of KwaZulu-Natal offers exhilarating encounters with sharks, rays and game fish. Lying 8km (5 miles) out to sea from the holiday town of Margate, its depth varies from 26–60m (85–200ft). Most dives take place at the Northern and Southern pinnacles – an area riddled with caves and overhangs where depths range from 30–60m (100–200ft) and 26–60m (85–200ft) respectively. Although the site is covered with many dainty invertebrates that attract a number of reef fish, divers mainly come here to see the sharks – crowds of raggedtooths invade the area during late winter and early spring, while the August sardine run brings copper sharks. The start of warmer weather coincides with the arrival of thousands of game fish which in turn attracts Zambezi and tiger sharks. Protea Banks is certainly not for the faint-hearted but it provides an unparalleled opportunity to dive with some of nature's most awe-inspiring creatures.

Previous pages Shoals of powderblue surgeonfish (*Acanthurus leucosternon*) are common on shallow reefs.
Opposite Boats are launched at Sodwana Bay's Jesser Point against a backdrop of forested coastal dunes.
Top Diving Aliwal Shoal involves a thrilling launch through the surf at the Umkomaas River mouth.

CLIMATE Nov–Jan hot, wet and humid; May–Jul cool and dry. Frontal systems from south may affect overall climate Jan–Mar.

BEST TIME TO GO *Sodwana* and *Aliwal Shoal* Year-round, reef conditions highly variable. Sharks Aug–Nov. *Protea Banks* Depends on type of shark you want to see.

GETTING THERE South African Airways (SAA) offer daily service from London's Heathrow and European locations to Durban via Johannesburg or Cape Town. Flights from US, Australia and the East too.

WATER TEMPERATURE *Sodwana* and *Aliwal Shoal* Average 22°C (72°F); cooler than elsewhere in Indian Ocean. *Protea Banks* 21°C (70°F) in winter.

VISIBILITY *Sodwana* and *Aliwal Shoal* Over 25m (82ft) Feb–Apr. Rain and river run-off affect visibility. *Protea Banks* 10–40m (33–131ft).

QUALITY OF MARINE LIFE *Sodwana* and *Aliwal Shoal* Great diversity, with some Indian Ocean species together with colder water species. *Protea Banks* Sharks, game fish (summer months) and rays.

DEPTH OF DIVES *Sodwana* 8–35m (26–115ft). *Aliwal Shoal* 5–30m (16–100ft). *Protea Banks* Fairly deep, 26–40m (85–130ft).

SNORKELLING Mabibi Lagoon, in 2m (6ft).

DIVE PRACTICALITIES *Sodwana* and *Aliwal Shoal* Minimum qualification NAUI Open Water I. *Protea Banks* Advanced divers only.

Sodwana Bay

Sodwana Bay is divided into a number of dive sites with names such as Two Mile Reef and Four Mile Reef indicating the distance from the access point; the closer the reef is to the shore, the more popular it is with the dive operators. Over 35,000 many juvenile fish tucked under overhangs, ribbontail rays can be found around the reef, while clown triggerfish display their spectacular coloration amid anthias, scorpionfish, moray eels and many species of parrotfish. Two Mile Reef is the largest reef in the system and is over 2km approach divers to within 8–10m (26–33ft). There are also large colonies of anemones, with attendant skunk clownfish, as well as Moorish idols and countless species of butterflyfish and angelfish. The inward edge of the reef offers protection to turtles and rays. The coral blocks are

divers visit the location every year, but the crowds tend to be localized and much of the remarkable coastline is virtually unspoilt. Each site has something special to offer and reefs such as Two Mile and Anton's are particularly popular due to the large schools of fish, primarily bigeyes and goatfish. This is fairly unusual and provides prime opportunities for photographers. Apart from the (1.2 miles) long and 900m (half a mile) wide, with depths ranging from 9–34m (30–112ft). Five Mile Reef is famous for the delicate miniature staghorn coral gardens that flourish there – trainee divers are not allowed here, however. Regular sightings of bottlenose dolphins are recorded at Seven Mile Reef. These graceful creatures betray their presence by their echolocation signals and will arranged in large buttresses and underhangs, testimony to the severe ground swells which occur periodically due to weather fluctuations off Madagascar and Mauritius.

One of the most striking features of these reefs is the number of cleaning stations – areas where tiny blue-and-white striped cleaner wrasse have set up shop to rid other fish of parasites and decaying

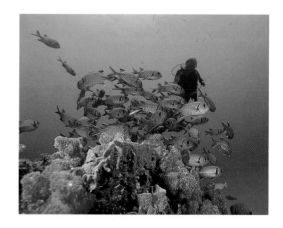

Above, left to right Generally found close to reef overhangs, glassy sweepers (*Pempherididae genus*) form massive schools which group together for protection from predators such as lionfish.

Left Potato groupers (*Epinephelus tukula*) are found on deeper stretches of the reef and around wrecks.

Right Silver soldierfish (*Myripristis melanosticta*) enjoy the shelter of reef ledges and caves.

skin. They will readily approach divers and signal their willingness to clean with jerky movements of the body combined with rapid flicks of the tail. Fish which are 'hunter' and 'hunted' often wait beside each other to be cleaned, as if someone had called 'half-time' in the game of survival.

Nearby Mabibi Lagoon contains a series of what can only be termed huge rock pools. These are exposed at low tide, the only time the area is accessible, and offer snorkellers and divers the opportunity to see a myriad fish. Inside the sheltered lagoon lurk octopus, electric rays, half-beaks, Picassofish, triggerfish, nudibranchs, bubble shells, blennies, gobies and lionfish. Tiny butterflyfish hide under the overhangs and hermit crabs scuttle about in brightly coloured shells.

On the landward side of the lagoon are huge sand dunes – some of the highest forested dunes in the world. The entire coastline is under the jurisdiction of the Natal Parks Board; permits are issued daily to restrict numbers on the beach and only 20 vehicles per day are allowed to travel along the beach, and then only at low tide so as not to endanger any turtle nesting sites.

Aliwal Shoal

The Shoal is a submerged rocky reef located approximately 5km (3 miles) offshore. All diving is by boat and while the ride from the launch site may only take 25 minutes, it may well provide as much excitement as the dive itself. Boats are launched at the mouth of the Umkomaas River and at certain times of the year, breakers meet the

downrush from the river over a series of sandbars resulting in 2–3m (6–10ft) waves. The local skippers are all vastly experienced and run the gauntlet of waves at breakneck speed; it is an exhilarating experience to say the least!

Apart from the many sharks, rays and dolphins, there are anthias, scorpionfish and lionfish, pixie hawkfish, Moorish idols and many species of butterflyfish and angelfish. At one time, the reef may have been home to a vast array of corals, but now these coralline limestone massifs are home to colonizing sponges and algal turf.

Of the wrecks in the area, two of the most interesting are the *Nebo*, which sank on 20 March 1884 while carrying bridge supports up the Natal coast, and the *Produce*, which hit the shoal on 11 May 1974. Both rest in approximately 30m (100ft) of water and provide refuge for many fish, invertebrates, eels, corals and sponges. The *Nebo* is also home to a pair of large brindle bass. Unfortunately, visibility around the wrecks is almost always poor due to the effluent discharge from the local Sappi Saiccor paper factory, which stretches for miles around. The problem is

Above A smooth grouper (*Dermatolepis striulatus*) stands ready to attack a shoal of sweepers.

Above right The common bigeye (*Priacanthus hamrur*) is a solitary inhabitant of coral caves.

Right Fingertip-sized cup corals (*Tubastrea* sp.) are found underneath archways, hidden from the sun.

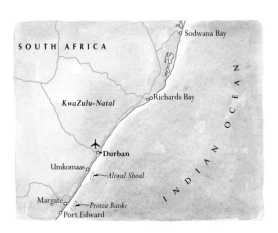

Below The Zambezi shark (*Carcharhinus leucas*) is seen on Protea Banks's deep reefs during summer.

following the inside ledge which connects the northern part of the reef to the southern part. The Southern Pinnacles has an average depth of 30m (100ft) and its varied topography includes caves and gullies – each favoured by different species of fish, both large and small.

For divers, the attraction of Protea Banks changes according to the season. Raggedtooth sharks arrive with the cooler countercurrents that flow over the bank during the late winter months and early spring. They congregate on the reef as part of their mating ritual, moving about sluggishly with their mouths agape. Scores of hungry predators invade the area during the August sardine run, while vast shoals of game fish – including barracuda, sailfish, wahoo, kingfish and jobfish – are brought to the banks by the easterly winds that cause thermoclines (layers of water of different temperature).

This signals the arrival of the Zambezi and tiger sharks. Although the Zambezi in particular has a dangerous reputation and is responsible for many attacks along the South African coast, underwater they seem almost shy of divers and never venture too close. Visitors to this remarkable site can also regularly see schools of hammerheads circling overhead like a flight of aircraft on a mission.

Above Lyretail anthias (*Pseudoanthias squamipinnis*) and golden cup corals (*Tubastrea aurea*) at the Shoal.

heightened during autumn (February to March), when the intensive inland rainfall causes silt and mud to pour out over the reefs; the temperature and salinity drop and the offshore winds can carry the sediment out to beyond the Aliwal Shoal. Undoubtedly, this silted freshwater run-off, combined with the industrial waste, has resulted in the strangulation of the once-pristine reef. A conservation group called the Aliwal Shoal Foundation is now active in trying to halt the decline and, if possible, reverse the damage.

Protea Banks

For years, Protea Banks was exploited by deep-sea fishermen and was a favoured hunting ground for several daring spearfishermen. However, while game fishing is still carried out, the region is increasingly becoming the preserve of sport divers for whom the thrill of swimming with huge schools of sharks is the main attraction.

This long sandstone reef is about 10km (6 miles) long and 0.5km (0.3 miles) at its widest part. Due to depth restraints, the reef is largely unexplored with divers tending to concentrate on a small stretch that is 4km (2.5 miles) long and 200m (650ft) wide. Starting at the Northern Pinnacles, a site only for the experienced, divers move south,

Opposite Divers swim around the hull of the *Nebo*, which is richly endowed with golden cup corals.

Below The raggedtooth shark (*Odontaspis taurus*) has a fearsome reputation due to its vicious teeth.

Below and far left During late winter and early spring, raggedtooths can be seen on the reef.

SEYCHELLES

Islands of Granite Boulders

L'ILOT · WHALE ROCKS · BRISSARE ROCKS · SHARK BANK · *ENNERDALE* WRECK

CLIMATE Varied, with distinct seasons marked by shift of monsoons; southeast monsoon blows mid-May–Oct. Highest rainfall Dec–Jan, hottest months Mar–Apr. Temperatures average 27°C (80°F).

BEST TIME TO GO Good year-round, although some sites affected by oceanic surge. Apr–Dec has best weather as well as SUBIOS, the underwater film festival.

GETTING THERE Air Seychelles has several flights per week, connecting with a number of European cities. British Airways offer two nonstop flights from London per week. Air France, Kenyan Airways and South African Airways also have services.

WATER TEMPERATURE Rarely drops below 27°C (80°F), even during winter.

VISIBILITY Best Apr–May and Oct–Nov (also calmest seas). Can drop during November with rise in plankton levels, which brings manta rays and whale sharks.

QUALITY OF MARINE LIFE Diverse and rich, although schools of fish not as vast as in Maldives. Many invertebrates of interest to photographers and marine biologists.

DEPTH OF DIVES Seychelles cover huge area, so anything from 20–50m (65–165ft).

SNORKELLING Many beaches protected by barrier reef creating safe shallow lagoons ideal for snorkelling. Also superb in St Anne National Marine Nature Reserve, Baie Ternay Marine National Park and Port Launay Marine National Park.

Comprising over 100 islands, the Seychelles lie four degrees south of the equator in the western Indian Ocean, northeast of Madagascar and some 1610km (1000 miles) east of Africa. The main island of Mahé, along with the islands of La Digue, Praslin, Denis, Bird, Aride, and Silhouette and numerous smaller outcrops, are collectively known as the inner islands. Cocos, the Amirantes, Poivre, Desroches, and remote Aldabra are referred to as the outer islands.

The unspoilt Seychelles are all that remained when Africa split away from India in the Precambrian period over 650 million years ago. Consisting almost entirely of granite, the main islands have little or no fringing reef for protection. Bird and Denis islands to the north are the only true coral islands within the main group. Like the Galápagos Islands, the volcanic origin and oceanic isolation of the Seychelles has guaranteed the preservation of a vast number of unique species of animals and plants, including a large population of giant tortoises on Aldabra atoll. The Valleé de Mai, a World Heritage Site located on Praslin, is home to many ancient forest specimens, as well as a number of rare or endemic birds including the black parrot with its distinctive cry. Compared to the Garden of Eden, the valley is the only place in the world where the erotically shaped coco de mer (*Lodoicea maldivica*), or 'forbidden fruit', grows. The shape of the nut resembles the female pelvic region.

Touching down on Mahé, the largest and most populated island, one is struck by the relaxed and hospitable atmosphere. The capital, Victoria, is clean and friendly, and still has a Saturday open-air market. The town's rich, harmonious mix of architectural styles reflects the amazing racial diversity of the local people, who are descended from Europeans, Indians, Asians and Africans, among others.

The name 'Seychelles' is enough to conjure up alluring images of palm-fringed white sandy beaches, crystal-clear waters and brightly coloured tropical fish and with over 900 species of fish, 100 types of shells and 50 varieties of coral, diving is an underwater photographer's delight. It is hardly surprising that SUBIOS, the annual Indian Ocean Underwater Film Festival, is held here. Minimal currents, abundant fish, colourful corals, and an above-average chance of seeing large pelagics such as manta rays, turtles and whale sharks, all make Seychelles a top destination. Most of the diving is from a boat, and the majority of the sites are a 10–20-minute ride from the shore. The dive centres all offer instruction in several languages, as well as equipment hire and escorted dives.

While the diving throughout the Seychelles is world-class, Aldabra is the jewel in the crown. The logistics of trying to dive the largest atoll in the world, however, restrict many divers. Although diving by boat is permitted, landing on Aldabra is forbidden as it is a World Heritage Site.

Opposite The approach to St Pierre Island is a fitting introduction to the Seychelles' boulder-strewn beauty.

Top Located 320km (200 miles) southwest of Mahé, the Amirantes comprise coral cays, islets and atolls.

L'Ilot

The tiny granite outcrop of L'Ilot, at the exposed tip of Beau Vallon Bay at North Point on Mahé, is a spectacular site bursting with marine life. Although the current between L'Ilot and the mainland tends to be quite strong, the small cluster of boulders in the centre yields one of the highest densities of marine life imaginable and is not to be missed. Golden cup coral festoons the canyons and gullies, while gorgonian sea fans, sea whips and other soft corals abound. Several Spanish dancer nudibranchs complete with symbiotic shrimps have been sighted on night dives, all within 1m (3ft) of each other, and in November it is here that divers and snorkellers regularly have the opportunity to swim alongside majestic whale sharks.

Above Shoals of indigenous Seychelles squirrelfish (*Sargocentron seychellense*) hide in branching coral by day and come out to feed by night.

Left Bluestriped snapper (*Lutjanus kasmira*) are always on the move, congregating in mixed shoals.

Whale Rocks

Situated to the south of Beau Vallon Bay, the huge granite blocks called Whale Rocks are a special spot where unique white gorgonians and fields of huge plate anemones, each with their own skunk anemonefish, reside. Golden cup corals and colourful bryozoans (or sea mats) reside in the shady areas, together with spiny lobster and various species of shrimp. The spotted snake eel, which is actually a member of the conger eel family, is an active feeder around these rocks at night; during the day, it hides under the sand.

Brissare Rocks

Virtually smothered in fire coral, which inflicts a nasty burn, this exposed offshore pinnacle is home to countless species of fish, including Napoleon wrasse, as well as eagle rays. Schools of parrotfish and wrasse intermingle with snappers, grouper and enormous aggregations of chromis and fusiliers. There are also large stands of staghorn coral where sweetlips and squirrelfish hide in the shadows. Nurse sharks are a regular occurrence and can be found 'sleeping' under the overhangs.

Shark Bank

Situated approximately 8km (5 miles) northwest of Mahé, Shark Bank is a massive granite plateau in approximately 30m (100ft) of water. As its name implies, sharks are frequently spotted in the area, although large stingrays are more commonly seen these days – especially around the boulder outcrops. These coral-encrusted boulders are a natural focal point for all divers, particularly photographers, as they teem with fish life not normally associated with the main island. One example is the cowfish; although fairly common at this site, it is rarely seen around Mahé. Pincushion starfish, with symbiotic shrimps on their shells, are also frequently spotted.

Ennerdale **Wreck**

This ship sank on a sandbar after striking an uncharted rock, 11km (7 miles) from Victoria in 1970. Lying in three sections in 30m (100ft) of water, the crumpled bows of the *Ennerdale* tend to have a congregation of stingrays and small whitetip reef sharks. As you descend to the wreck, the water column soon becomes crowded with large shoals of batfish and onespot snapper, which vie for your attention. The tangled superstructure is quite interesting and, being easily accessible, allows for relatively safe exploration. Dives tend to be around the stern section which is mostly intact; the wheelhouse and propellor are both readily accessible as well.

DIVING THE AMIRANTES

Situated approximately an hour's flying time, or 320km (200 miles), southwest of the main Seychelles group, the Amirantes were known to Persian traders centuries long before Vasco da Gama sighted them in 1502. Originally known as the Admiral's Islands, they comprise some 17 coral cays, islets and atolls, most barely inhabited and many leased for private use or for the cultivation of coconuts.

The large island of Desroches offers some of the best diving. Situated on the southern side of a huge atoll, the diving off the wall is indeed spectacular with dramatic caverns, caves, tunnels and overhangs. The ancient limestone reef has been sculpted by waves and weather over the centuries, creating a backdrop to scuba diving which is quite unlike any elsewhere in the Seychelles. On entering the water, divers are engulfed by schools of oriental sweetlips and Bengal snapper. The larger openings on the reef top form tunnels which are linked to the outer reef; sightings of nurse sharks and moray eels are common in these tunnels. Approaching the outer reef wall, divers are met by large stands of black coral and brilliant red sea fans, all of which have longnose hawkfish in residence.

Opposite top The emperor angelfish (*Pomacanthus imperator*) is common around all of the islands.

Opposite bottom, and above The visibility in the Amirantes' caves and caverns is usually spectacular.

Right A diver pauses to inspect the marine activity in a cave entrance off Desroches in the Amirantes.

MALDIVES

Magical Realm of Atolls

ARI ATOLL • FELIDHU ATOLL • LHAVIYANI ATOLL • BAA ATOLL

The Maldives consist of an extensive chain of 26 atolls lying off the tip of India some 670km (415 miles) west of Sri Lanka. The approximately 1195 low-lying coralline islands within the Maldives archipelago rise from a common submarine platform that plunges to depths of up to 4000m (13,120ft) in places. Thanks to the mid-oceanic position of this large plateau, far away from the effects of pollution and silt-filled estuaries, an infinite variety of marine species prospers under near-perfect conditions in this natural aquarium.

One's first impression of the Maldives is of a vast expanse of ocean out of which small patches of land protrude; in fact, much of the country lies just below the water's translucent surface, and crossings by boat between atolls are consequently largely restricted to daylight hours. Built atop one of the largest reef systems in the world, these atolls have become a magnet for snorkellers and scuba divers who relish the opportunity to drift for extended periods above shallow reef crests. The fish which reside on these shallow reefs are unusually tame, and include tang, butterflyfish, angelfish, and surgeonfish. The friendliness and approachability of these myriad reef fish is a hallmark of diving in the Maldives.

Tourism, which started developing rapidly in the 1970s, expanded outward from Hulule, an island which is part of a large central atoll known as Malé. Hulule soon became a natural hub as a result of the international airport located there. As the demand for more exclusive lodgings and unspoilt dive sites grew, resorts sprang up on each little island in the atoll. These days there are over 75 resort islands to choose from on a range of atolls, from South Malé, Ari and Rasdhu to Felidhu, Lhaviyani, and even Baa. A three- or four-hour boat ride from the airport island to some of the newer resorts is not uncommon. Each resort island has access to an average of 40 different dive sites, excluding remote spots accessible by live-aboard operations only. As well as diving, snorkelling, sailing and windsurfing, the resorts offer a wide variety of other sporting activities, including volleyball and tennis; some even have fully equipped gyms.

Diving in the Maldives is site-specific, however, which means that you cannot just enter the water anywhere and expect to see reefs blanketed with corals and fish. Indeed, like most of the world's best-known dive destinations, the Maldives boast many exceptional sites scattered amid miles of more modest reef. Due to the immense size of the archipelago, exploring huge reef lines for isolated treasure troves can be a formidable and expensive pastime. The quality of the dives is therefore completely dependent on the resort and the motivation of the local dive operator to take divers to the best sites. A live-aboard cruise offers the obvious benefit of gaining access to sites that are as yet untainted by daily boatloads of divers.

Opposite The Shipyard is easy to locate as the bow of one of the wrecks clears the surface of the water.
Top The Maldivian atolls were formed when ancient volcanoes subsided, leaving behind circular reefs.

CLIMATE Affected by seasonal monsoons. Northeast monsoon (Nov–Apr) is hot and dry, southwest monsoon (May–Oct) brings wind and rain. Average temperatures 24–30°C (75–86°F). In general, days are hot and humid.

BEST TIME TO GO Year-round, although Mar–Apr visibility good, seas calm and skies bluest. European high season Nov–Feb.

GETTING THERE Charter flights to Hulule airport on Malé atoll from South Africa and Europe. Regular flights from Far East and Sri Lanka. Most live-aboard operations and hotels arrange transfers.

WATER TEMPERATURE Varies between 26°C (79°F) during rainy season (May–Oct) and 30°C (86°F) during dry months (Nov–Apr).

VISIBILITY Excellent year-round, although affected by currents and plankton blooms; averages between 20–40m (66–131ft).

QUALITY OF MARINE LIFE Over 1000 fish species and a wide array of invertebrates. Highlights include moray eels, manta rays, grey and whitetip reef sharks, barracuda, brightly coloured soft corals and sea fans.

DEPTH OF DIVES Maldivian law prohibits divers from diving below 30m (100ft).

SNORKELLING Superb. Most resorts have a house reef, easily accessible from beach.

DIVE PRACTICALITIES Qualified divers to produce proof of certification.

Above Collare butterflyfish (*Chaetodon collare*) are commonly found on rocky sections of the reef.

Left The beautifully patterned honeycomb moray eel (*Gymnothorax favagineus*) feeds at night.

A wealth of different diving opportunities exists within the Maldives' reef system. Shallow protected lagoons contained within atoll rims provide shelter for delicate corals and small reef fish which thrive on the nutrient-laden currents that stream in and out of the atolls through tidal passes. These deep channels cut through the reef structure, linking the lagoons to the open sea. Some passes are so narrow that you can see from one side right across to the other. Inflowing water from the open sea is usually clear, while the outflowing current picks up suspended matter as it is carried towards the opening, thereby reducing visibility. Some of the best dive spots in the Maldives occur at tidal passes, since it is the flow of microscopic particles on outflowing currents that causes these sites to flourish. Dives can be timed to coincide with periods of slack water rather than full-flood tides to moderate the effect of the currents. Manta rays hover in the channels with gaping mouths, filtering the rich water; soft corals and sea fans extend their tiny polyps into the current; and gaudily coloured butterflyfish, angelfish, goatfish, fusiliers, and fairy basslets are often seen. Tilas, which are outcrops of calcified coral on the channel floor, represent thriving reef communities. Thickly covered in vivid soft corals,

they are often visited by sharks, rays, turtles and other pelagics that are drawn in from the open sea by the intense food stream. Beyond the lagoons, the outer walls of the reef plunge down to immense depths. Exposed to the forces of the open sea, coral growth on these slopes is fairly limited although the fish life is diverse and prolific.

ARI ATOLL
Kudarah Tila
Located in a channel between the two fishing islands of Dangethi and Dhigurah on the southeastern rim of Ari Atoll, this is probably one of the best tilas in the Maldives; it is small enough to encircle several times during one dive. Covered in a profusion of soft corals of every imaginable colour, the tila also attracts an enormous school of bluebanded snappers that sway gently in the current. At the end of a dive, you can float over the reef top with its anemones and clownfish.

Haa Alifu Atoll
Haa Dhaalu Atoll
Shaviyani Atoll
Noonu Atoll
Raa Atoll
Lhaviyani Atoll
Baa Atoll
Kardiva Channel
Kaafu Atoll
(North Malé Atoll)
Rasdhu Atoll
Malé
Alifu Atoll
(Ari Atoll)
Kaafu Atoll
(South Malé Atoll)
Vaavu Atoll
(Felidhu Atoll)
Faaf Atoll
Dhaalu Atoll
Meemu Atoll
Thaa Atoll
Laamu Atoll
One and Half Degree Channel
Gaafu Dhaalu Atoll
Gaafu Alifu Atoll
INDIAN
Equatorial Channel
OCEAN

Halaveli Wreck
This purpose-sunk wreck lies near the reef of the resort island of Halaveli on the northeastern side of Ari. Resting on the sand bed at 28m (92ft), the boat is home to several stingrays that come out to greet you as you descend to the site.

Fish Head and Maayafushi
Lying in the northern secton of Ari Atoll, these sites were once popular for shark feeds. Although the sharks are no longer fed by dive instructors, they still gather at the sound of approaching boats.

FELIDHU ATOLL
There is a spectacular pass on the northeast side of Felidhu near Foteo Island which brings together several facets of Maldivian diving. The tilas are shallow (5–9m; 15-30ft) and the entire channel perhaps 55m (180ft) wide. On the ocean side there is an abrupt drop-off from about 12m (40ft)

Above In dim light anemones often close up, shutting out their anemonefish and damselfish.

Right Juvenile threespot damselfish (*Dascyllus trimaculatus*) associate with large anemones.

Below Tiny pink eggs are visible inside the body of a transparent cleaner shrimp (*Periclimenes* sp.).

to some 21m (70ft), before the wall falls away to the distant ocean floor. The western side of this precipice is graced with four small caverns, one above the other. The walls and ceilings are covered with colonies of orange, yellow and cream-coloured soft corals, creating magical interiors which are so immense, a photographer would be hard-pressed to capture them.

LHAVIYANI ATOLL

The Shipyard

On the western rim of Lhaviyani, close to Felivaru Island, lie two shipwrecks offering interesting diving opportunities. The rusting bow of the *Skipjack I*, which protrudes above the water, is a focal point in the area; the vessel sank during a storm in 1980. The second wreck was sunk by its owners a few months later. Swept by rich currents, the wrecks have become the foothold for large soft corals while encrusting sponges and algae fight for space on the ships' hulks. Reef fish swarm over the site, which is accessible from the resort island of Kuredu.

BAA ATOLL

The countless sites on remote Baa Atoll used to be the sole domain of live-aboard boats until the construction of a resort on Sonevafushi Island on the southern rim of the atoll. Now this pristine area overflowing with marine treasures is fast becoming one of the Maldives' prime dive spots.

Above and left Exposed to the elements, the rusting bow of *Skipjack I* belies the magical realm beneath the water where hard and soft corals, sponges and algae cover every inch of the wreck.

SOUTH & WESTERN AUSTRALIA

Great White and Whale Sharks

DANGEROUS REEF • NINGALOO REEF

CLIMATE *Dangerous Reef* Unpredictable, can change from 24°C (75°F) to 12°C (54°F) with 74kph (40-knot) winds a few hours later. *Ningaloo Reef* Brief two-month season (mid-Mar–May) with generally beautiful weather, 26–28°C (78–83°F).

BEST TIME TO GO *Dangerous Reef* Feb–Mar for fine weather. *Ningaloo Reef* Arrival of whale sharks triggered by coral spawning each March; the effect lasts 6–8 weeks.

GETTING THERE *Dangerous Reef* Fly to Adelaide, transfer to live-aboard boat. *Ningaloo Reef* Fly to Perth, then north to Learmonth. Coastal town of Exmouth 25 minutes by bus from Learmonth.

WATER TEMPERATURE *Dangerous Reef* 17–21°C (62–69°F). *Ningaloo Reef* Normally 27–29°C (80–84°F).

VISIBILITY 5–12m (15–40ft) at *Dangerous Reef*, up to 18m (60ft) at Neptune Islands. Varies at *Ningaloo Reef*, 18–30m (60–100ft).

QUALITY OF MARINE LIFE Great white sharks major. attraction at *Dangerous Reef*. *Ningaloo Reef* Whale sharks legendary; other sharks also found. Kangaroo Island for leafy sea dragons.

DEPTH OF DIVES *Dangerous Reef* Cages from just below the surface to 27m (90ft). *Ningaloo Reef* Surface to 18m (60ft). Diving suitable for all qualified divers.

SNORKELLING *Dangerous Reef* Possible in cages to see sharks, if no baiting is going on. *Ningaloo Reef* Superb with whale sharks.

In the diving world there are some destinations, and certain experiences, that are unique. The great white sharks of South Australia's Dangerous Reef and other similar reefs, and the majestic whale sharks of Ningaloo Reef are two of these legendary places.

In February 1976, the first group of sport divers flew to Adelaide, South Australia, specifically to dive with great white sharks. What followed was a series of hair-raising expeditions led by famous Australian diver, Rodney Fox. These early experiences had a major impact on the sport and, every year in February, divers still make the pilgrimage to South Australia. The select few who have been down in cages to observe the great white shark form one of the most exclusive clubs in the diving world.

Ningaloo Reef, a 161km-long (100-mile) fringing reef which lies along the outer perimeter of the remote Northwest Cape some 1930km (1200 miles) north of Perth in Western Australia, is the location of annual whale-shark sightings. The tiny outback town of Exmouth and the airstrip at Learmonth are the only specks of civilization on the sparsely vegetated coastal plain. Each year in March, in accordance with the phases of the moon, countless reef-building coral polyps release their eggs and simultaneously spawn into the sea. This event triggers a fascinating feeding cycle. Before the appointed day, masses of shrimp-like

krill are drawn to the coast in anticipation of the feast. The filter-feeding whale sharks are not far behind, sifting through the plankton-filled waters for krill with their vacuum-like mouths.

Diving at Ningaloo Reef demands a fair amount of organization. A spotter plane is hired to circle above the reef. The whale sharks swim 90–180m (295–590ft) off the reef and it is the pilot's job to radio the boat's captain as soon as a shark is seen off the reef's perimeter. Once the instructions have been received, the captain steers the boat towards the shark, while divers scramble to don their gear and ready their cameras. According to law, divers have to be dropped well clear of the whale shark. In the days leading up to the spawning, the spotter plane can fly the length of the reef and not see a single whale shark. Yet on the day of the spawning, the same flight path may yield 20 of them.

As with the great white sharks, each whale shark has a distinct personality. Some swim purposely in search of the next krill mass, while others, perhaps having eaten their fill, will amuse themselves by investigating the puny divers they encounter. For the divers, they are moments of pure magic as they share a dance with these effortless swimmers. With a few lazy sweeps of their barn-door-sized caudal fins, the whale sharks eventually leave the divers in their wake and disappear into the blue.

Opposite Ningaloo Reef in Western Australia is famous for its whale shark (*Rhinocodon typus*) sightings.
Top A great white shark (*Carcharodon carcharias*) swims close to a shark cage at Dangerous Reef.

Dangerous Reef

From a practical standpoint, mounting an expedition to film or view great white sharks is straightforward – the devil is in the details. Basic requirements include a substantial ship, large cages, and tons of bait. To feed their bulk, great white sharks

need whole sea lions or other marine mammals; South Australia's offshore sea lion colonies are made to order. Locales such as Dangerous Reef, North and South Neptune islands and Little English and Sibsey islands have all yielded classic sightings in the past. Dangerous Reef is sometimes closed to dive operations for months at a time to protect the sea lion colonies.

The bait that is lowered into the water briefly diverts the sharks from their stalking of sea lions. Thinking perhaps that the boat is a dead whale leaking blood, the sharks are drawn from kilometres away. Their approach is unpredictable, and often startling. The adventure begins the moment the first shark appears out of the gloomy ocean depths. Great white sharks are massive and perfectly formed, and the very sight of one of these secretive predators can alter the viewer's personality. Each shark exhibits its own singular behaviour. Some pass by in majestic review, observing the divers in their suddenly inconsequential cages with studied insouciance. Others move in swiftly with barely contained ferocity, watching for the slightest hint of how they might penetrate the cages to reach the humans within. Those great white sharks that stalk the cages show the same patience, guile and single-mindedness one would imagine them exhibiting when chasing a sea lion. There is, however, no hint of the Hollywood vengeance that drove the mythical *Jaws* creature; all that is fantasy.

Great whites are being mortally threatened by humankind. Slaughter by accident in tuna nets or on purpose by vengeful humans, is drastically reducing their numbers. Those who have stared into a shark's great black eyes hope that they will continue to haunt the seas, but there is no assurance that they will endure. It would be our loss were these shadowy presences to fade away.

Above and right A great white shark (*Carcharodon carcharias*) displays its impressive teeth while trying to attack the mass of bait used to attract it.

Ningaloo Reef

Once a dive boat is in close proximity to a whale shark, the captain parallels the animal's course from a distance. Sometimes a member of the crew will hop overboard and snorkel in the vicinity of the shark, acting as a marker of its course and speed. Then the captain will ease the boat well forward of the shark, cross its path and shout 'Now!' At the sound of his voice, bodies fly overboard in the divers' rush to descend in the shark's path. Upon impact with the water, each

diver hurries to get below the surface by perhaps 5m (15ft). Moments later, like a mothership in outer space, the broad unmistakable head of the whale shark materializes out of the haze. In the best encounters the shark will slow down and swim right up to the divers. In the past, a shark would sometimes swim right up to a diver so that it could be gently patted on the forehead or stroked beneath the mouth. When touched on the dorsal or pectoral fins, however, the whale shark lowers its head and powers away.

Left and below Dwarfed by their massive size, divers give scale to these majestic whale sharks (*Rhinocodon typus*) with their enormous gills.

Above A close-up of a whale shark's vacuum-like mouth, which is designed to filter-feed thousands of krill and small fish at any one time.

To avoid that kind of harassment, the authorities of Western Australia have instituted a 'no-touch' policy and as a result, divers can now enjoy longer and easier encounters with these gentle creatures. A well-run dive boat and spotter plane may yield 10 or more shark dives each day; some divers have been lucky enough to swim with 17 in a single day, and up to 45 in six days! That is a lot of whale sharks by any measure, and accounts for the genuinely legendary status of this stretch of Western Australia's desolate coastline.

INDO-PACIFIC

THAILAND

Kingdom of Soft Corals and Pelagics

KOH SIMILAN NATIONAL PARK • KOH SURIN NATIONAL PARK • PHUKET DAY TRIPS

Covering over 500,000 km² (193,000 sq miles), Thailand is an independent kingdom that has retained a strong sense of national identity and traditional culture over the centuries. The majority of tourists head for southern Thailand (where the Isthmus of Kra separates the Andaman Sea from the Gulf of Thailand), which stretches from the capital, Bangkok, down to the border with Malaysia. Most of the popular resort islands are in the Gulf of Thailand to the east of the mainland, and in the Andaman Sea to the west. The top dive sites, however, and the majority of diving services, are concentrated in the Andaman Sea. Although the Gulf of Thailand does offer diving opportunities, the visibility and marine life tends to be far better off the west coast.

Thailand's vibrant cultural life is just one of many attractions for the visitor. The creative skill of the Thais is evident not only in classical Thai music and dance but in a wide range of crafts as well. Thai food is a veritable feast for the eyes and the palate. Buddhism, the religion of 90 per cent of the nation, manifests itself in elaborate temple architecture and an easy-going attitude best summed up by the phrase *mai pen rai*, which means 'no worries'. Buddhist temples, rainforests and beautiful tropical islands with unpolluted swimming beaches have also contributed to the country's position as the top tourist destination in the region, with some five million annual visitors.

The range and variety of sites in the Andaman Sea is enormous. There are spectacular open-ocean sea mounts; dramatic granite outcrops plunging into the depths; caves, tunnels and swim-throughs to explore; extensive fringing reefs and fabulous drop-offs. Some 30 genera and well over 100 species of fish have been recorded, as well as over 200 species of coral. Many of the reefs have suffered from blast fishing, but the growth in dive-related tourism and the increased protection afforded by the revenue it has generated is now helping to offset the damage caused in the past.

Phuket is the main centre for diving in southern Thailand, and it is here that you will also find the greatest range of accommodation, from five-star luxury resorts to simple beach huts. Unfortunately, the coral reefs immediately surrounding the island are only used for training dives these days, due to the damage they suffered in the past. Frequent live-aboard excursions to the Koh Similan, Koh Surin and Koh Lanta national parks depart from Phuket, as do numerous day trips to some excellent offshore sites situated an hour or two away by boat.

Some 50km (30 miles) southeast of Phuket, Koh Phi Phi and its neighbouring islands offer a variety of shallow reefs, pinnacles and caverns, as well as fascinating limestone walls which plunge down into the depths and are festooned with feather stars, gorgonians and barrel sponges.

CLIMATE Dominated by northeast and southwest monsoons in southern Thailand. From May–Oct, southwest monsoon brings heavy rains and strong winds to Andaman Sea. Year-round temperatures vary between 21–34°C (70–93°F).

BEST TIME TO GO Between Nov–Apr when Andaman Sea calm and visibility better.

GETTING THERE Phuket has international airport with scheduled and charter services to and from Europe and Asian countries. Phuket can also be reached overland by train, bus or long-distance shared taxi from elsewhere in Thailand.

WATER TEMPERATURE Averages 27–31°C (75–88°F).

VISIBILITY Best between Nov–Apr; ranges from 5–30m (16–100ft).

QUALITY OF MARINE LIFE Good, despite some areas being overfished. Ranges from colourful gobies to massive groupers and pelagics (manta rays, sharks, tuna, and even whale sharks). Rare species include the dugong, found around Koh Lanta.

DEPTH OF DIVES Fringing reefs start in around 5m (16ft) of water or less; drop-offs and granite outcrops drop down to 100m (330ft) or more.

SNORKELLING Excellent around offshore islands, with the exception of Phuket (reefs poor). Snorkelling equipment available for rental, as are traditional longtail boats for trips to offshore sites.

Previous pages Porcelain crabs (*Neopetrolisthes* spp.) have a commensal relationship with sea anemones.
Opposite Weathered, softly rounded granite boulders epitomize the landscape on the island of Similan.
Top A live-aboard vessel and a local fishing boat find a suitable overnight anchorage in a protected cove.

Some of the best diving in the Andaman Sea is in the Koh Similan and Koh Surin national parks. With thriving fringing reefs and dramatic underwater topography, these two groups of islands offer a wide range of spectacular dive sites.

South of Phuket, beyond Koh Phi Phi, lies the relatively unexplored Koh Lanta National Park with excellent sites such as Hin Daeng, a wall dive packed with sharks, and Hin Mouang, a series of submerged pinnacles.

Koh Similan National Park

Covering an area of 128km² (51 sq miles), the Koh Similan National Park is a popular destinations for live-aboards from Phuket, and is widely considered to be one of Asia's top diving destinations. The Similan group lies some 90km (55 miles) northwest of Phuket, and consists of nine small granitic islands with stunning white sand beaches on their eastern shores and rugged boulders rising up directly from the sea bed on their western shores. In the past, the Similans have suffered from blast fishing and bottom trawling, but the enforcement of national park regulations has largely curtailed these practices and the reefs and marine life have had a chance to regenerate and are once again thriving.

The above-water topography is reflected in the park's underwater terrain. Dive sites on the eastern leeward coasts generally encompass fringing reefs and walls descending to a rock and sand sea bed. The sheltered conditions and moderate depths make these sites suitable for any level of diver; snorkelling is also at its best in east-facing bays. The western shores, by contrast, feature giant boulders which drop down to depths of 40m (134ft) and beyond; the gaps between these boulders are swept clean by southwesterly currents and provide a maze of swim-throughs, archways and tunnels. The currents also provide nutrients for the mass of vibrant soft corals,

crinoids and gorgonian sea fans which cling to the jumbled boulders' surfaces. Beyond the immediate shoreline, there are more granitic boulders that form giant pinnacles and plateaus where many large pelagics congregate.

During late-March and April, the hottest months, the teeming fish populations of the Similans are augmented by large numbers of pelagic visitors such as whale sharks, manta rays, large barracuda, tuna, and jacks, as well as eagle rays.

Some of the most popular dive sites within the Koh Similan National Park include Fantasea Reef, which is a mass of towering boulders featuring numerous caverns, arches and gullies; Elephant Head, or Hin Pousar, with its fabulous swim-throughs and masses of hard and soft corals; and Beacon Beach Reef, a fringing reef that is also very popular with snorkellers.

Koh Surin National Park

Located some 53km (48 nautical miles) northeast of the Similans, the Koh Surin National Park comprises five granite islands clad in spectacular primary forest. Underwater, most of the dive sites follow gently sloping fringing reefs alive with butterflyfish, angelfish and parrotfish, bluespotted ribbontail rays, tangs and a species of wrasse.

Left, from top to bottom An emperor angelfish (*Pomacanthus imperator*) and a sixspot grouper (*Cephalopholis sexmaculata*) hover over the reef; a pair of cuttlefish (*Sepia pharaonis*), photographed at Richelieu Rock, has the ability to change the patterns and markings on their skin depending on their surroundings; lionfish (*Pterois volitans*), known as turkeyfish in America, have beautiful fronds that carry a powerful sting; a striking clown triggerfish (*Balistoides conspicillum*) hides from a diver behind a huge barrel sponge (*Xestospongia testudinaria*).

Outside the national park boundaries, 14km (7.5 miles) to the east, is Richelieu Rock, one of Thailand's most famous dive sites. Consisting of one large submerged pinnacle surrounded by several smaller ones, Richelieu Rock is a magnet for pelagics such as trevally, snappers, tuna and barracuda; it is also one of the best locations in Thailand for sightings of the magnificent whale shark, the largest fish in the ocean.

Phuket Day Trips

One of the most popular day trips from Phuket is to Anemone Reef, a completely submerged pinnacle with rocky ledges covered in carpets of sea anemones as well as huge gorgonian sea fans and vibrant soft corals. Groupers, moray eels and lionfish take shelter around its flanks.

Above A longnose hawkfish (*Oxycirrhites typus*) hides in the camouflaged safety of a gorgonian sea fan.

Right Masters of disguise, frogfish (*Antennarius* sp.) mimic sponges in their quest for obscurity.

Below Among *Tubastrea* coral, tasselled scorpionfish (*Scorpaenopsis oxycephala*) are darker in colour.

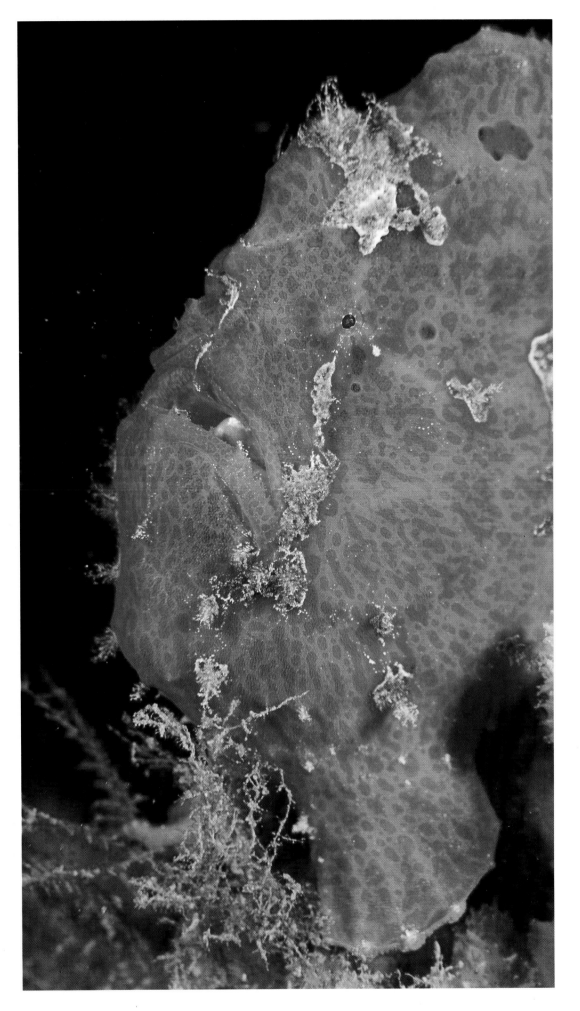

Nearby Shark Point (Hin Musang) forms part of the same marine sanctuary. This small outcrop features a wealth of marine life including brilliant soft corals, gorgonian sea fans, hard corals, groupers, numerous lionfish, giant barrel sponges, jacks, barracuda, snappers, and moray eels.

Koh Dok Mai, a small islet 90 minutes from Phuket, has limestone cliffs that plunge vertically into the depths with gorgonian sea whips, barrel sponges and hard corals on the reef wall providing shelter for a rich variety of reef fish. Blacktip and whitetip reef sharks are often spotted around the western side of the island. Visibility at these offshore sites is usually unpredictable.

Above Young whale sharks (*Rhinocodon typus*) are often encountered by divers at Richelieu Rock.

Left A diver's perspective of thousands of tiny fish fry which effectively blot out the sun.

Above Almost obscured by a massive shoal of fry, a young whale shark is trailed by a photographer.

Right A shoal of fusiliers (*Pterocaesio* spp.) dashes through an undersea valley off the Similan Islands.

CLIMATE Tropical with two main seasons; warm and humid year-round. Temperatures 26–30°C (80–86°F) except on high ground. Only Peninsular Malaysia's northeast coast affected enough to warrant closing down offshore tourism during monsoon period. Otherwise, strong winds rare.

BEST TIME TO GO Peninsula's east coast drier Apr–Oct; wetter season Nov–Mar. Pulau Sipadan year-round, but is calmest and driest May–Oct.

GETTING THERE Flights to Kuala Lumpur, with connections to Pulau Tioman; onward land or ferry transfers to other islands. For Pulau Sipadan, flights to Kota Kinabalu in Sabah, then to Tawau. Transfer to island by helicopter or by speedboat from Semporna.

WATER TEMPERATURE Average 25°C (77°F) in cooler season and 31°C (88°F) in warmer season in deep water. Average 30°C (86°F) in shallow water.

VISIBILITY Sipadan approaches mythical 60m (200ft); rarely below 30m (100ft). Other sites vary 3–30m (10–100ft).

QUALITY OF MARINE LIFE Diverse and prolific, often very tame and inquisitive. Large pelagics often encountered inshore.

DEPTH OF DIVES Most are suitable for all standards of divers. Some dives at Sipadan descend to depths greater than sport divers should dive, so act responsibly.

SNORKELLING Excellent from the shore or in shallow water over coral reefs.

MALAYSIA

The Land Where Two Winds Meet

PULAU SIPADAN MARINE RESERVE

Situated in the heart of Southeast Asia, Malaysia is a confederation of 13 states and two federal territories. Geographically, it consists of two distinct regions separated by 500km (310 miles) of the South China Sea. The 805km-long (500-mile) Malay Peninsula extends from the border of Thailand in the north to Singapore in the south. Across the sea, in Borneo, are the Malaysian states of Sarawak and Sabah, together with the federal territory of Labuan.

With attractions such as beautiful national parks and reserves, orang-utan and turtle sanctuaries, the world's largest flower (the rafflesia), empty beaches, and pristine reefs, it is clear why the Malaysian government enthusiastically promotes ecotourism. The country also exhibits a fascinating ethnic and cultural diversity. Despite the images this may conjure up, all modern communications are available – even on tiny, remote islands such as Sipadan.

Most of the undeveloped parts of Peninsular Malaysia are covered in tropical rainforest. On the west coast, long fertile plains descend from the central mountain range to the sea, which is dotted with resort islands such as Penang and Langkawi. The eastern side descends more steeply with beautiful white sand beaches that shelve gently into a turquoise sea. Underwater, jumbles of large boulders are carpeted with corals and sponges and as you dive deeper, sea fans, soft corals, and harp and black corals can be seen. In general, the marine life and its rate of growth is prolific. Pulau Tioman and Pulau Perhentian Besar are two of the islands off the Peninsula's east coast which have thriving beach resorts and professional dive operations. Pulau Redang, Pulau Aur and Pulau Tenggol, which have more stony corals and less sand, are potential world-class diving destinations.

Over in Borneo, off the west coast of Sabah, Labuan's shipwrecks are a haven for marine life and wreck fanatics. Whale sharks arrive in numbers off Kota Kinabalu between January and April. The remote Layang-Layang and Spratly islands have sheer walls, strong currents and large pelagic species, but at depths only suitable for experienced divers.

Pulau Sipadan, a 12ha (30-acre) island covered with tropical rainforest and fringed with sandy beaches, lies 35km (22 miles) off Semporna on Sabah's east coast. The ultimate dive site, it offers everything from the easiest shore diving to drifting with currents, night dives, and deep walls; turtles are also a highlight. All diving is undertaken from small boats or from the beach. With a feast of diving concentrated inshore, live-aboards have not been successful. The shallow reef crest has vast fields of colourful corals teeming with approachable reef fish, invertebrates and turtles. The walls are thick with sponges, sea fans, corals, nudibranchs, crabs, and lobsters. Shoals of jacks, barracuda, fusiliers and bumphead parrotfish charge about while pelagics patrol the deep.

Opposite In contrast to its extensive fringing reefs, Pulau Sipadan comprises a mere 12ha (30 acres) of land.
Top Lying off the Peninsula's east coast, Redang is a tropical island paradise with rainforest-clad sandy shores.

PULAU SIPADAN MARINE RESERVE

Just north of the equator, Pulau Sipadan is perched on a volcanic sea mount, with its walls rising abruptly from depths of 600m (1969ft). Divers began venturing here in the late 1970s, but it was only in 1988 that Borneo Divers obtained permission for permanent accommodation which was opened in 1989. In the same year, legendary undersea adventurer Jacques Cousteau arrived with the research vessel *Calypso*. 'I have seen other places like Sipadan, 45 years ago, but now no more. Now we have found an untouched piece of art', were his prophetic words.

With more than 200 species of fish and over 70 genera of corals, the marine life off Pulau Sipadan equals Australia's Great Barrier Reef for species diversity. Large areas of pristine stony corals are interspersed with soft corals, anemones and sponges. The walls are festooned with sea fans, black corals, *Dendronephthya* soft corals, and colourful *Tubastrea* and *Dendrophyllia* species. Colourful crinoids spread out in the currents. The waters teem with turtles and inquisitive shoals of fusiliers, barracuda, batfish, catfish, sweetlips, jacks, goatfish, and bumphead parrotfish.

Above Female turtles come ashore at night to lay their eggs on the beach. When the eggs finally hatch out, the turtle hatchlings head for the sea under cover of darkness in order to minimize predation.

Left Although endangered, green turtles (*Chelonia mydas*) are plentiful in the waters surrounding Pulau Sipadan. They can be observed feeding, resting and mating (particularly during October).

Jetty Beach and Drop-off

This has got to be the world's best beach dive, and a top night dive. Shoals of small fish and invertebrates characterize the reef top while over the drop-off, a huge shoal of jacks and smaller shoals of sweetlips and batfish circle. Deeper down, among overhangs and caverns, divers come across angelfish, leaf fish, lionfish, butterflyfish, scorpionfish, map pufferfish, orangestriped and clown triggerfish, spotted and Vlaming's unicornfish, Moorish idols, moray eels, nudibranchs, sea squirts, and sponges.

Map labels:
Barracuda Point
Coral Gardens
Jetty Beach & Drop-off
Turtle Cavern
Whitetip Avenue
North Point
Beach Huts
PULAU SIPADAN (Malaysia)
Turtle Beach
Lagoon
Mid Reef
West Ridge
CELEBES SEA
Hanging Gardens
Turtle Patch
Lobster Lairs
Staghorn Crescent
South Point

TURTLE CAVERN

The famous turtle cavern is romanticized as the place where turtles go to die; in reality they become lost in the dark interconnecting passages and drown (below). The caverns were formed as a result of weathering during the last ice age when sea levels were around 100m (330ft). The main entrance, a large cavern on sand at 18m (60ft), descends to 21m (70ft). At the back of this cavern, a tunnel leads to a smaller cavern that interconnects with others rising to less than 4m (13ft) from the surface. The dark caverns are also home to shoals of flashlightfish, as well as shrimps and crabs that have adapted to the gloomy conditions. This advanced dive requires a divemaster as a guide, as it is possible to get dangerously lost.

Barracuda Point

Featuring a shallow reef top sloping gently down to the northernmost point of the sea mount's east face, a huge shoal of barracuda, reef sharks, garden eels and turtles are found at this site where divers should expect strong currents.

Coral Gardens

This is a shallow dive above the crest of the sea mount's northeast face where vast fields of corals teem with fish, including a huge shoal of bumphead parrotfish. It is truly an underwater photographer's paradise.

Whitetip Avenue, Mid Reef and Turtle Patch

The centre of the east face has a colourful reef crest, rich in stony and soft corals and vibrant reef fish as well as giant clams and turtles. Down the wall in deeper water there are huge sea fans, large barrel sponges, soft tree corals and black corals. Turtles congregate at Turtle Patch further south.

South Point, Staghorn Crescent and Lobster Lairs

The southern end of the reef is similar to Barracuda Point. Currents can be strong and often change direction. Large shoals of fish, manta rays, eagle rays, turtles and sharks are common. Lobsters hide in crevices at Lobster Lairs.

Hanging Gardens, West Ridge and North Point

The west face to North Point has a shallow crest covered in corals and anemones teeming with associated fish. Over the drop-off, the wall features plenty of overhangs containing *Tubastrea* and *Dendrophyllia* corals, sea fans, black corals, and barrel sponges, hence the name 'Hanging Gardens'. Nudibranchs, flat worms and crinoids also abound at this site.

Right, top to bottom Sipadan's rich marine wonderland includes the bumphead parrotfish (*Bolbometopon muricatuni*), which uses its forehead to break off coral; the scorpionfish (*Scorpaenopsis* spp.), adept at varying its colouring to blend in with its environment; squirrelfish (*Holocentridae* spp.); and bigeye trevally (*Caranx sexfasciatus*).

PHILIPPINES

Great Species Diversity

TUBBATAHA REEFS · JESSIE BEAZLEY REEF

Strategically separating the South China Sea from the Pacific Ocean, the Philippines lie south of Taiwan, east of Vietnam, northeast of Borneo and north of Indonesia. Scientists believe that the triangle formed by the Philippines, Peninsular Malaysia and Papua New Guinea is where most of the Pacific's marine organisms evolved before spreading out to colonize other oceans. The area certainly has the widest variety of marine species in the world.

With around 7107 islands and islets, of which only 2000 are inhabited, the Philippines forms the world's second largest archipelago after Indonesia. The islands stretch approximately 1850km (1150 miles) in a narrow north-to-south configuration, and span 1100km (680 miles) east to west. The irregular coastline with its stunning palm-fringed beaches borders almost 34,000km² (13,124 sq miles) of coral reefs.

During the 1980s, the Philippines went through a period of destructive blast fishing, as a result of which the international diving community lost interest. All this has changed, and international hotel chains and dive operators have invested extensively in the tourist industry. Education and employment opportunities have helped prevent the local people from ruthlessly destroying the reefs. Aided by warm waters and strong currents, soft corals and *Acropora* stony corals are growing extremely fast, and many reefs are visibly regenerating – albeit with different species.

Dive operations in the Philippines vary from those attached to international resorts to small operators situated on sleepy beaches who rely on walk-in trade, although all are based in exceptionally scenic locations. In fact, many people visit these shores as much for the world-class dive sites as for the magical surroundings above water. Boracay's White Sand Beach is listed among the world's 10 best, Cebu is renowned for its holiday beaches, and the beauty of Puerto Galera and Coron have to be seen to be believed.

Most diving is from small outrigger boats, called *bancas* in the local language. Apart from the Tubbataha region, live-aboard diving is in its infancy, although this is fast changing with the demands made by serious divers. Quality wreck diving can be experienced in Subic Bay, now open after being closed to divers by the American Naval Base. There is also an impressive Japanese fleet from World War II in Coron Bay.

The reefs in the Philippines have typically shallow reef tops covered with barrel sponges, sea fans, stony corals, soft corals, and hydroids, and swarm with fish. Along the walls, shoals of curious angelfish, pennantfish, Moorish idols, fusiliers, and sweetlips, among others, follow you. Pelagics, including sharks, rays and turtles, are also seen. Caves contain resting nurse sharks. Whitetip reef sharks, spiny lobsters, nudibranchs, flat worms, sea cucumbers, sea stars, sea squirts, featherduster worms, and colourful crinoids are everywhere.

CLIMATE Tropical, with distinct seasons. Average temperature 23–36°C (73–97°F). Dry season Nov–Feb; wet season Jun–Oct when typhoons can occur in the north. Northeast monsoon blows Nov–Mar; gentle southwest monsoon blows Jun–Nov.

BEST TIME TO GO Year-round for most areas, although Apr–May reliably calm throughout archipelago; Tubbataha Reefs only comfortably dived Mar–Jun.

GETTING THERE Fly to Manila or Cebu. Philippine Airlines have onward domestic flights to all major destinations including Puerto Princesa from where live-aboard boats head for Tubbataha Reefs.

WATER TEMPERATURE 25–31°C (77–88°F).

VISIBILITY Generally excellent; 40m (130ft) plus on flood tide.

QUALITY OF MARINE LIFE Diverse and prolific. Large pelagic species regularly encountered on offshore reefs.

DEPTH OF DIVES Many open-water reefs descend to depths greater than sport divers should dive, so act responsibly.

SNORKELLING Good snorkelling from shore or in shallows above coral reefs from *bancas*, or live-aboard tenders.

DIVE PRACTICALITIES In open water strong currents common, especially at spring tides. Novices to be accompanied by experienced divers on Tubbataha Reefs. Equipment hire and courses offered.

Opposite A diving *banca* awaits clients on Panglao Island's beautiful Alona Beach, creating an idyllic scene.
Top Most sites are accessed by local outrigger *bancas*, which have been adapted to cater to divers' needs.

115

TUBBATAHA REEFS

Diving on the Tubbataha Reefs, situated 182km (113 miles) southeast of Puerto Princesa on Palawan Island, is strictly from a live-aboard boat. Together with Jessie Beazley Reef, these reefs make up the Tubbataha Reef National Marine Park. The Tubbataha Reefs are actually two extensive atoll-like reefs, known as North and South reefs, with inner lagoons separated by a channel that is approximately 7km (4 miles) long. At low tide several sand cays are visible. At the northeast end of North Reef is Bird Islet, a sandy cay with grass and mangroves. Brown boobies and terns occur here, and turtles nest on the beach.

South Reef has a prominent black rock and some sandy cays at the northeast end, as well as a solar-powered lighthouse where gulls and terns nest. High and dry on the reef, to the east of the lighthouse, is the wreck of the *Delsan*.

North Reef

A rich slope of corals on sand descends from 14–20m (45–65ft) at North Reef, followed by a wall with overhangs, caves and crevices, which descends deeper than sports divers should go.

The reef top, rich in lettuce, staghorn, table, leathery and whip corals, and sponges, teems with fish. Trumpetfish, cornetfish, anthias, Napoleon wrasse, damselfish, clownfish with associated anemones, angelfish, lionfish, scorpionfish, boxfish, groupers, triggerfish, pufferfish, hawkfish, and parrotfish abound. Guitar sharks, sea stars, sea urchins, sea cucumbers, segmented worms, garden eels, featherduster worms, and nudibranchs decorate the sand, and colourful crinoids sift through the current for food particles. Below 30m (100ft), there are soft corals and enormous gorgonian sea fans. Large pelagics patrol the wall while manta rays and turtles are common near the surface.

South Reef

This reef has a sloping reef top to between 10–20m (33–65ft), and a richly endowed wall down to depths which are beyond the capabilities of most sports divers. The wall is covered in gorgonian sea fans and barrel sponges similar to those at North Reef; the soft corals and pelagic species are even better. Eagle and manta rays are common while sea grass attracts turtles.

Jessie Beazley Reef

SULU SEA

TUBBATAHA REEFS (Philippines)

Bird Islet

North Reef Lagoon

South Reef Lagoon

Black Rock

Delsan Wreck

Lighthouse

Jessie Beazley Reef

At this prime dive site, there is a rich coral slope from 5–10m (16–33ft), followed by a sheer wall which descends to some 40m (130ft) before sloping out into the depths. The reef top, covered in lettuce and leathery corals, is dense with reef fish. Most striking here are large shoals of fish that follow you around. There are unusually large numbers of sabre squirrelfish, bigeyes, snappers, jacks, Vlaming's unicornfish, rainbow runners, emperors, pennantfish, batfish, and sweetlips. Triggerfish, groupers and hawkfish hang around and at the western end, grey reef and whitetip reef sharks rest on the sand at the base of the wall. Every hole houses a redtooth triggerfish, and manta and eagle rays are commonly seen.

Top left The coral grouper (*Cephalopholis miniata*) is one of the most colourful fish on the reef.

Below right A spawning crown-of-thorns sea star (*Acanthaster planci*) in a classic arched position.

Above Colonies of strangely contorted stony corals (*Pachyseris rugosa*) grow in an upright position.

Above A blue tube sponge (*Aplysina* spp.) is one of many bright sponges that grow in these waters.

Above left A sea fan (*Gorgonian ventalina*), bubble coral (*Plerogyra sinuosa*) and feather star on the reef.

On all three reefs, currents vary from gentle to fierce and unpredictable, and may change during the course of a dive. Drift diving from live-aboard tenders is the norm. A high-visibility late deployment surface marker buoy or rescue tube should be carried to attract the attention of your chase boat. The season is short and the weather can be rough, so pick your boat with care. Serious divers and photographers must visit these reefs.

Above A large shoal of bigeye trevally (*Caranx sexfasciatus*) circles slowly at the reef edge.

Right Sunlight streaming through a hole in the roof gives Gunther's Cathedral a spiritual quality.

Above Red feather stars (*Himerometra robustipinna*) feed by opening their arms to collect plankton.

INDONESIA

Diving the World's Largest Archipelago

PULAU SILADEN • SACHIKO'S REEF • MANADO TUA 1 • RAYMOND'S REEF • MANDOLIN REEF • FUKUI

CLIMATE Two distinct seasons; clear skies, hot during dry season (May–Sep), heavy rain during wet season (Nov–Mar). Average year-round temperature 29–31°C (84–88°F), with lows 6°C (11°F) cooler.

BEST TIME TO GO Apr–Oct, although superb year-round.

GETTING THERE International airports in Jakarta, Denpasar and Kupang offer same-day connections to Indonesian destinations; Manado airport in Sulawesi has flights to and from other Southeast Asian countries. Resort operators arrange local transfers.

WATER TEMPERATURE Usually 26–27°C (78–80°F); local upwellings and seasonal variations can lower it by 5–6°C (9–10°F).

VISIBILITY Excellent; 25–30m (80–100ft), sometimes 50m (165ft) or more.

QUALITY OF MARINE LIFE Spectacular; reefs densely packed with incredible coral and huge numbers of reef and pelagic fish. Also turtles, dolphins, whales and dugongs.

DEPTH OF DIVES All depths to 30m (100ft). Deeper dives can be planned by those with suitable experience level.

SNORKELLING On shallow inshore reefs close to beach in most areas. Dive boats accept snorkellers for offshore trips.

DIVE PRACTICALITIES Dive certification required. Equipment hire and dive tuition available at most shore-based resorts and on some live-aboards.

Composed of over 13,000 islands, ranging from tiny, uninhabited islets to large landmasses, Indonesia is a nation of immense diversity. In the past few decades, the spectacular bounty of its coral reefs has come under increasing pressure from overfishing and other human activities, and there is a pressing need to sustain Indonesia's reefs so that divers may continue to enjoy this exceptional underwater realm.

Indonesia is in the centre of the Indo–Pacific biosphere, one of the richest and most diverse marine habitats on earth. By comparison with other temperate-water dive sites, Indonesia's reefs are as colourful, and alive with countless species more familiar in tropical aquaria than from previous diving experiences. Diving here can be equated with plunging into the pages of a fish encyclopaedia; in fact, a guide to tropical reef fish was researched and photographed in these waters. The conditions are exceptional with visibility consistently in the 25–30m (82–98ft) range during the hot dry season. Although the water is very warm, a thin neoprene suit is advisable, not least for protection from the many stinging hydroids.

Grouper, or rock cod, lurk in caves and crevices, while large shoaling reef fish patrol the reef. These include red and black snapper, various species of surgeonfish and unicornfish, as well as pelagic visitors such as glittering jacks and trevally. The big end of the spectrum is shared by bulky bumphead parrotfish, stately Napoleon

wrasse and giant grouper, with sharks and rays of several species a common shadowy presence. Huge tuna, sleek barracuda and Spanish mackerel cruise in from the open sea to feed on the rich pickings provided by the abundant reef species.

Besides fish, mammals such as dolphins, several types of whale and the elusive dugong all make their homes in these waters; leatherback, green and hawksbill turtles, and several sea snakes are also common in Indonesia.

Coral growth is as diverse as the fish life, with hundreds of species identifiable on some reefs – a profusion of hard and soft corals that defy description. Branching stony corals, star and brain corals, lettuce and plate corals, gorgonian sea whips, pulsing *Xeniids* and brightly coloured *Dendronephthya* – these are just a fraction of the numerous species on offer in these waters.

A definite highlight of diving in Indonesia is Bunaken–Manado Tua Marine Park, a marine reserve of over 75,000ha (185,000 acres) only a few kilometres offshore from Manado. Besides the tiny island of Manado, the reserve encompasses Bunaken, Manado Tua, Montehage, and Nain. Each island is surrounded by a dense coral reef which makes the naming of individual sites almost pointless. Diving in the Bunaken area is without exception wall diving on sheer vertical coral walls with phenomenal growth well into the depths. Fish life is diverse and includes all the common reef species, as well as sharks, rays and turtles.

Opposite A small fishing boat is silhouetted against a glorious sunset backdrop over Manado Tua Island.
Top Boats, such as this one off Manado Tua near Manado, are the local form of transport in Indonesia.

Pulau Siladen

This island is situated about 3km (10 miles) northeast of Bunaken. Accessed by boat, the dive site is a vertical wall packed with thousands of coral ledges. The overall effect is a bit like a fish supermarket, with something different on every shelf. Rich reef shallows feature perfectly formed coral heads, while profuse coral growth continues over the drop-off and down the wall to the depths. An exceptional variety of fish species prevails, with the small creatures of the reef top contrasting with the larger varieties off the reef face and in the deep blue; bumphead parrotfish, the odd Napoleon wrasse, barracuda and grey reef sharks, big schools of unicornfish, snapper, trevally, and surgeonfish are just a few examples of what there is to see. From large fish to dense packs of schooling species, colourful reef species or tiny invertebrates and reef rarities, this spot has it all.

Sachiko's Reef

Situated on Bunaken's north shore and accessed only by boat, Sachiko's (named after a Japanese tour guide) is a vertical hard and soft coral wall with an interesting profile of shelves, undercuts, overhangs, canyons, valleys, caves, cavelets, and chimneys which drop away from reef flats full of small reef fish and dazzling corals. Small and medium reef fish reign supreme. In particular, there are dozens of species of butterflyfish, as well as trumpetfish, grouper, snappers, sweetlips, hundreds of angelfish, and any other reef species your heart desires. Grey and whitetip reef sharks are also common, and tend to add the finishing touch to a truly memorable dive.

Manado Tua 1

This site off the southwest coast of Manado Tua incorporates tremendous variety in terms of profile and contour, as well as fish and coral in many permutations. The reef runs from a shallow reef top to a deep reef wall characterized by cavelets, overhangs, shelves, ledges, and valleys and bays. There are stony and hard coral forms ranging from spiky *Acropora* to velvety *Dendronephthya*.

Left Colourful feather stars, out feeding during the day, are a common sight on South Pacific reefs.

Raymond's Reef

With only a slight current, this site off the west coast of Bunaken, opposite Manado Tua, is perfect for drift diving. Its main feature is a spectacular wall, which is undercut in places, covered in corals and frequented by large whitetip reef sharks, turtles, grouper, sweetlips and huge schools of snapper. Crystal-clear waters provide an unobstructed view into the depths. The site offers a perfect blend of larger wall fish and smaller coral-dwelling species that reside on the sheltered reef top, which is between 2–5m (7–16ft). Coral growth and fish life are abundant up on the reef top, with damselfish and basslets of all descriptions, many in jewel-bright colours, covering the coral heads.

Mandolin Reef

Located a few hundred metres off the southwest coast of Bunaken, Mandolin Reef comprises a vertical wall that faces Manado Tua. A wide, flat reef top, dense with corals and tiny reef fish, extends out from the shore for 200–300m (656–984ft), providing scope for snorkellers. The site's exposed location at the tip of a reef 'peninsula' means that it is affected by strong currents, but it also draws large pelagics and schooling species such as trevally, barracuda, monster dogtooth tuna (some weighing up to 100kg, or 220 pounds) and swarms of snapper, unicornfish and surgeonfish. Grouper and rock

cod stand out among the dense population of reef fish, which includes dense concentrations of pyramid butterflyfish. Big whitetip reef sharks and banded sea snakes, moray eels, smaller tuna in the 90cm (3ft) range, and turtles are all frequently spotted at this site as well.

Fukui

This sloping reef on Bunaken's south coast has more corals than any north Indonesian site. Its stepped profile is marked by an abundance of *Acropora* table corals. Brain, lettuce, elkhorn, staghorn, lace and needle corals, and a number of soft coral species make up just a tiny fraction of the coral growth on offer, which is all complemented by shoaling and pelagic fish in their thousands, as well as countless reef species.

Above Brain and acropora corals have specifically evolved to withstand strong currents, though they can be damaged by typhoons and hurricanes.

Right, from top to bottom A blennie is extremely hard to spot, since it is usually well camouflaged; this hawkfish is resting on a basket star; a goby, with characteristic protruding eyes, on a soft coral; a brittle star clings to a black coral; a brightly coloured hingebeak shrimp (*Rhynchocinetes hiatti*).

Map labels: Nain Island; Montehage Island; CELEBES SEA; INDONESIA; Raymond's Reef; Pulau Siladen; Manado Tua Island; Sachiko's Reef; Bunaken Island; Manado Tua 1; Fukui; Bunaken Village; Mandolin Reef

PACIFIC OCEAN

PAPUA NEW GUINEA

Rare and Wonderful Species

MILNE BAY • NORTHERN ISLANDS • EASTERN FIELDS

The large, multifaceted nation of Papua New Guinea includes the eastern half of New Guinea, an island in the western Pacific, north of Australia, as well as a scattering of smaller islands and archipelagos to the north and east of it. The mountainous, rainforest-clad shores of these islands were probably the reason why Papua New Guinea was one of the last corners of the world to be explored by European navigators in the 17th century.

Partly because of the islands' rugged terrain and inherent remoteness, Papua New Guineans have retained numerous aspects of their primitive culture. Local tour operators offer cruises up the Sepik River and treks into the Highlands, a unique opportunity to experience this inimitable culture – one that will not last forever as tourism invades these once isolated shores. Accommodation along the way is in comfortable lodges.

Papua New Guinea's legendary dive sites, which are scattered over literally thousands of miles of ocean, reveal an astonishing variety of offbeat, often endemic marine species, including species of leaf fish and lionfish, and numerous species of clownfish. Due to the country's small dispersed population, the fishing pressure on its marine resources has been relatively modest and, as a result, many of its dive sites also yield reliable encounters with schools of jacks and barracuda, as well as turtles and sharks.

Diving in Papua New Guinea started with a single live-aboard, the *Telita*, which began operating in Milne Bay at the eastern tip of New Guinea. Before long, excited reports of chambered nautilus, gaudy Merlet's scorpionfish, and other equally unusual species led to a cult-like diving movement.

The success of these early diving cruises led inevitably to further live-aboards, which began operating among the far northern islands of New Ireland and New Hanover; at astonishing sites southwest of Port Moresby in the northern reaches of the Coral Sea; and among the Hermit and Ninigo island groups. Despite the high cost and the long flights, Papua New Guinea has fast become the Pacific's ultimate diving destination – even for the most jaded of divers.

There are few experiences more thrilling than being almost alone on a site such as Banana Bommie or Dinah's Beach and finding one rare species after another – mandarinfish, which are also found in the Philippines, Indonesia and Papua New Guinea, mantis shrimps, and brilliant red *Premnas* clownfish and razorfish.

In the future, as the demand to dive world-class sites increases, larger dive cruisers will no doubt replace the original 10-passenger vessels of New Guinea's awakening. Some will consider this progress, others a loss. With luck and thoughtful management, these dive sites and their exciting species will thrill divers for generations to come.

Previous pages Longfin batfish (*Platax teira*) usually swim in small shoals and regularly surround divers.
Opposite Outrigger canoes in Papua New Guinea have one outrigger; in the Philippines they have two.
Top Papua New Guinea is characterized by inaccessible mountainous terrain cloaked in dense vegetation.

CLIMATE Tropical, but highly variable; cool and windy conditions Jul–early Oct, frequent rain showers Jan–Mar.

BEST TIME TO GO Year-round destination for live-aboards, though water warmer and weather more preferable mid-Oct–Jun.

GETTING THERE Flights to capital Port Moresby via Sydney, Hong Kong, Manila and Singapore; Port Moresby has some reasonable hotels for overnight stays before transferring to live-aboard boat for Coral Sea and Eastern Fields cruises. To Milne Bay, a one-hour flight from Port Moresby to Alotau is necessary; to northern islands, a three-hour multiple-stop flight to Kavieng.

WATER TEMPERATURE 26°C (78°F) Jul–Aug, 28–29°C (82–84°F) Nov–May.

VISIBILITY Milne Bay 15–27m (50–90ft); deep-sea sites reach 30m (100ft) or more. Kavieng 15–38m (50–125ft). Best site is Eastern Fields, usually 46m (150ft) or more. Plankton blooms possible late Nov–Dec.

QUALITY OF MARINE LIFE Superb, great variety and many rare species (scorpionfish, ghost pipefish and mandarinfish). Especially attractive destination for photographers.

DEPTH OF DIVES From surface to 43m (140ft); best diving in 21m (70ft) or less.

SNORKELLING Very good, although only some sites have suitable shallow reef tops.

DIVE PRACTICALITIES Boat owners deliver divers to sites that match their level of skill.

Milne Bay

Milne Bay, a live-aboard destination accessed from Alotau on the mainland, is as singular as more famous sites in the Pacific such as Cocos Island or Truk Lagoon; it is a genuine phenomenon in the diving world. Divers who have completed several 10-day cruises to Milne Bay find that they are still discovering new species on every trip. For underwater photographers, this is the ultimate qualification for a famous destination. The Milne Bay region is blessed with hundreds of different dive sites; some are right off secluded mainland beaches, while others are remote specks of shallow green reef in a blue sea. Considered among experienced divers to be choice sites are Dinah's Beach, where the term 'muck dive' was first defined – a dive site that at first may look ugly and unappealing, yet is alive with unusual underwater finds; Banana Bommie, a large current-swept pinnacle at the mouth of Milne Bay which enjoys a profusion of species from spider crabs to barramundi cod; Observation Point, another muck dive, with resident mandarinfish and ghost pipefish; and See and Sea Reef, a shark and big-animal site. Divers with patience and sharp eyes will be rewarded with glimpses of Merlet's scorpionfish and other fascinating

Below The leaf scorpionfish can change its colour from pale yellow through bright red to dark brown.

Above A fine close-up of a Merlet's scorpionfish (*Rhinopias aphanes*) showing its deadly dorsal spines.

Below A vibrant red leaf scorpionfish (*Taenianotus triacanthus*) mimics a leaf rocking in the current.

Above A well-camouflaged weedy scorpionfish (*Rhinopias frondosa*) lies motionless waiting for prey.

marine treasures. Besides small rare species, Milne Bay is just as likely to have sharks, pilot whales, rays or turtles. On the odd occasion, marlin and crocodiles have been photographed from live-aboard boats such as the *Telita*.

Northern Islands

The sea surrounding the islands of New Hanover and New Ireland, which are situated to the north of the mainland, teems with large pelagic species. Several of these sites, such as Chapman's Number Two, the Fish Place and Silvertip Reef, offer reliable encounters with schooling barracuda, giant groupers, schooling jacks, large dogtooth tuna, occasional manta rays, and whale sharks.

While New Hanover does have some classic muck-diving sites, serious divers are more intent on acquiring rare photos of big, dramatic animals in the wild. When you have clear-water conditions here, the results can be spectacular.

Silvertip Reef alone is worth the entire trip; a half-dozen fat and sassy silvertip sharks move into the area as soon as the anchor rattles down. During the preparatory dive, they parade before

Below The spiny devilfish (*Inimicus didactylus*) lies motionless to ambush small fish and crustaceans.

Below The harlequin ghost pipefish (*Solenostomus paradoxus*) blends in with gorgonians and crinoids.

Below The cockatoo waspfish (*Ablabys taenianotus*), like the leaf scorpionfish, mimics swaying leaves.

the cameras, patient in the certainty of the rich feed to come. The second, feeding, dive is an all-out extravaganza with a wealth of sharks.

Eastern Fields

There are numerous dive sites around Eastern Fields, an atoll 138km (86 miles) southwest of Port Moresby in the Coral Sea. One, in particular, has become known as Carl's Ultimate Reef due to the immense richness of life surrounding this massive undersea structure. It swarms with enormous schools of barracuda, jacks, rainbow runners, fusiliers, *Heniochus* bannerfish, and tuna, as well as sharks, turtles and giant groupers. Impressive 1.5m-tall (5ft) trees of soft coral, 3m-high (10ft) gorgonian sea fans, and countless dancing fairy basslets complete the picture on this reef.

Above The peppermint-striped sea cucumber (*Thelenota rubrolineata*) has distinctive papillae, and moves along the reef by means of tube feet.

Opposite A miniature imperial shrimp (*Periclimenes imperator*) finds camouflaged refuge on a Spanish dancer nudibranch (*Hexabranchus sanguineus*).

Left This Spanish dancer species (*Hexabranchus imperialis*) is so called because the white rim of its mantle resembles the flamboyant skirts of a flamenco dancer.

Right This cowrie has taken on the exact colours and shape of its home, a gorgonian sea fan.

Above, clockwise from top left Pink anemonefish (*Amphiprion perideraion*), common clownfish or clown anemonefish (*Amphiprion ocellaris*), saddleback anemonefish (*Amphiprion polymnus*), common clownfish, spinecheek anemonefish (*Premnas biaculeatus*), common clownfish. Anemonefish, often called clownfish due to their gaudy colouring and erratic behaviour (they charge and grunt at other fish and divers), are members of the damselfish family and live commensally with anemones.

Opposite In dim light, the *Heteractis magnifica* anemone closes tightly, leaving its companion, an attendant pink anemonefish (*Amphiprion perideraion*), outside.

MICRONESIA

Sites of Enduring Interest and Fame

PALAU ARCHIPELAGO • TRUK LAGOON • YAP ISLAND

CLIMATE Humid and warm with frequent brief showers. *Palau* rainy and windy in summer; *Truk Lagoon* often windy in winter.

BEST TIME TO GO *Palau* is best Oct–early Jun. *Truk Lagoon* a year-round site, although photographers prefer Jan–May. Nov–May for the rays in *Yap*, although a different channel has rays May–Nov.

GETTING THERE Air Micronesia flights from Guam, Manila (Philippines) or Palau. Most operators provide airport transfers.

WATER TEMPERATURE Ranges between 27–29°C (80–84°F); coolest Jul–Sep.

VISIBILITY At flood tides, *Palau* can reach 46m (150ft) on outer walls. At out-flowing tides, turbid lagoon water reduces visibility to 15–24m (50–60ft). *Truk Lagoon* Highly variable, usually 18–24m (60–80ft).

QUALITY OF DIVING Best sites range from sheer walls in crystal-clear water, to World War II wrecks, caverns, blue holes, and shallow coral gardens.

DEPTH OF DIVES *Truk Lagoon* From surface to over 46m (150ft). Best wrecks in 21m (70ft) or less; there are deeper wrecks for more advanced, experienced divers.

SNORKELLING Best at *Palau* due to shallow reef tops. *Truk Lagoon* When visibility good, snorkelling can be sublime.

DIVE PRACTICALITIES Level of experience required by divers depends on the site.

To get even a vague idea of the true extent of Micronesia's 7.8 million km² (3 million sq miles), a glance at a Pacific map reveals that it starts just west of Hawaii and ends due south of Tokyo. Most of that expanse is open ocean, punctuated here and there by colourful atolls and archipelagos. The quality of diving varies greatly in Micronesia and sites are widely dispersed; as a result, live-aboard boats are highly favoured, especially since they cut out commuting time and offer the chance to explore the waters around many isolated, and therefore unspoilt, atolls. Whether you choose the convenience and luxury of a live-aboard or not, there are a number of locales in Micronesia of enduring interest and fame, including Palau, Truk Lagoon and Yap.

There are those who insist that the softly rounded, plush-green islands of the Palau, or Belau, archipelago are the most beautiful in the Pacific. Between the islands, shallow sand flats gleam aquamarine under a high sun and divers are completely enchanted before they even drop into the water.

Koror, the capital and site of the airport, is more or less centrally located in the Palau archipelago. The most famous dive sites are a bumpy 32km (20-mile) or more boat ride south of the capital where a huge channel, the Ngemelis Pass, cuts through the main barrier reef. The trip takes at least an hour, even in perfect weather. Here, some of the most varied and magnificent reef topography in the Pacific region – sheer walls, huge 'blue holes' and inviting caverns filled with magnifent stalactites – is on proud display.

Islanders throughout the Palau archipelago are known for their extraordinary handiwork, which differs from one island to the next. Particularly striking are the storyboards depicting local legends, carved in exquisite bas-relief.

Truk Lagoon, the site of a World War II American attack on Japanese supply lines, boasts the world's largest aggregation of wrecks located at routine depths in benign, warm-water conditions. The documented American aerial bombardment of February 1944, which became known as Operation Hailstone, created a premier wreck-diving paradise for divers.

Over the years, as more divers made their way to Truk and Palau, other islands were discovered, and soon Air Micronesia's jets between Guam and Palau were stopping in Yap. Although the reefs are acceptable, divers touch down in Yap specifically to visit manta ray cleaning stations situated in channels where tidal waters flow in and out of the lagoon – a short boat ride from the only hotel.

In Ponape, or Pohnpei, the stone ruins of the mysterious 1000-year-old city of Nan Madol, together with the Kaprohi Waterfall, offer a fascinating diversion. The ancient city was built from 12m-long (40ft) basalt hexagonal columns which were quarried 64km (40 miles) away and transported to the site in canoes.

Opposite A view of some of the unforgettable, thickly wooded 'rock islands' for which Palau is well known.
Top A typical calm day at Truk Lagoon, final resting place of many Japanese warships from World War II.

PALAU ARCHIPELAGO

Although many of the sites in Palau are deep, there are also shallow reefs that allow unlimited diving. Excellent sites include the immense blue holes of Kayangel to the north and the current-swept corner in the Peleliu Islands, on the way to Papua New Guinea. What has drawn two decades of eager divers to Palau, however, are the five sites in the Ngemelis Pass area – the Ngemelis Wall, the Blue Corner, the Quadruple Blue Holes, and two lovely coral gardens.

Big Jellyfish Lake

This lake on the island of Eil Malk in Palau is home to an enormous school of mastigias jellyfish; it is believed that there are over two million of these creatures living in the lake's warm, salt waters. Because the jellyfish have no predators in the lake, they have lost their stinging tentacles. Swimming amid this pulsing multitude is a truly eerie experience for divers. It has been described as 'swimming in a bowl of clear jelly'.

Algae living in the jellyfishes' bodies are used to produce food by photosynthesis, compelling the animals to follow the path of the sun across the lake each day. At night, when there is no sun for photosynthesis to take place, they fall into the depths of the lake where rotting organic debris has rendered the water toxic. When the sun comes up again, the jellyfish rise to the surface.

Ngemelis Wall

From the air, the horseshoe-shaped indentation in the otherwise straight outer barrier reef surrounding the Palau islands and the lagoon is easy to spot. The shallow, sand interior of this indentation is furrowed by a die-straight, man-made waterway known as the German Channel. Were it not for this thoroughfare, which permits

Above and opposite Mastigias jellyfish (*Mastigias papua*) in Big Jellyfish Lake, one of five saline lakes on the island of Eil Malk in the Palau archipelago.

Right Smaller barracuda (*Sphyraena* spp.) school in colossal sociable armada at Palau's Blue Corner.

boats to travel south among the islands in fairly sheltered water, divers would have to approach the Ngemelis Wall from the open sea in difficult, potentially rough conditions.

The Ngemelis Wall is some 400m (a quarter-mile) long and straight as a rule. Its crest is a few feet from the surface, making it an attractive site for snorkellers. From the crest, the wall plunges vertically to beyond 60m (200ft) before levelling off to form the floor of the pass. Since substantial tidal currents flow along the wall, variable conditions are commonly experienced on different dives. As a result of this tidal flow, a profusion of gorgonian sea fans, sea whips, soft corals and sponges are attached to the wall. Away from the wall, impressive schools of jacks and barracuda can be seen, as well as shoals of parrotfish. Manta rays, sharks and other pelagics are also occasionally seen. From the top of the wall it is possible to snorkel over the reef shallows to a beautiful tropical island and beach.

Blue Corner

Situated around the seaward end of the Ngemelis Wall, this site comprises a roughly triangular-shaped, flat-topped promontory, which projects some 45–70m (148–230ft) into deep water. The same fast-moving tidal currents that sweep past the Ngemelis Wall provide rich feeding for soft corals and fans on the outer, deeper point of the promontory and also attract sharks as well as schools of barracuda to the Blue Corner.

Quadruple Blue Holes

Just beyond Blue Corner, four vertical shafts lead down from a depth of 1.5m (4ft) straight into a series of immense caverns which are open to the sea. Divers can swim down one of these shafts into the caverns and enjoy the huge black coral trees hanging from their roofs before returning up the outer wall. At high noon, at a depth of about 34m (110ft), shafts of brilliant sunlight pour down the Blue Holes, bathing divers in the dark caverns below in a halo of light.

PEARLY NAUTILUS

The pearly nautilus (Nautilus pompilius) makes daily nocturnal vertical migrations from abyssal depths – about 400m (1312ft) – to the shallows (left) where it scavenges on crustaceans. The interior of its spiralled shell is divided into a series of gas-filled chambers. As each nautilus grows, it creates a new

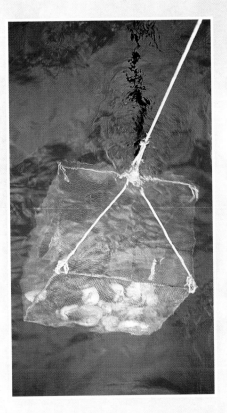

chamber with a wall of mother-of-pearl. By secreting and absorbing gas in these chambers, the animal is able to regulate its buoyancy and is thus unaffected by pressure changes. When a nautilus is captured in a wire cage (above) and brought to the surface for scientific study, or to be studied by divers, it is not harmed. It swims by jet propulsion, and in deep water is an aggressive scavenger.

TRUK LAGOON

All too many divers dismiss Truk Lagoon as a dive site they would expect to find repetitive and boring ('If you have seen one wreck, you've seen them all') but, in reality, each of the wrecks is surprisingly different. Many of the ships that sank here during World War II settled upright on flat sand. Today, the superstructures and decks of some of these wrecks are within 21m (70ft) of the surface, making several of them visible to snorkellers. Fed by constant currents bearing planktonic food, coral and fish have thrived on these metal reefs for more than 50 years. Lush, colourful soft-coral gardens have bloomed on certain of the wrecks, and today shallow dives on the *Shinkoku Maru*, *Yamagiri Maru*, *Fujikawa Maru*, and others present divers with coral gardens as opulent as those of the Red Sea and Fiji; indeed, some of the soft coral colonies which hang from cables and spars are among the largest in the world. Other wrecks, such as the *Gosei Maru*, lie in shallow water where there are no currents. These hulks are as stark and barren today as when death rained from the sky, and their broken hulls declare the futility of war with cosmic silence.

Below In clear water, the futility of war is captured in a ship's bow that will never again see the sun.

Right The immense architecture of the *Fujikawa* wreck creates vertical coral gardens.

YAP ISLAND

Yap, like Palau, is surrounded by an outer barrier reef. Two major channels furrowing through the reef allow vast volumes of tidal water to flow in and out of the lagoon twice a day. In these channels there are shallow shelves of sand and coral populated by juvenile butterflyfish and small wrasse. Practically every day, manta rays gather at these cleaning stations to have parasites and dead skin picked off their bodies.

The best way to view the mantas is to settle quietly, and unobtrusively, on the sandy bottom and wait for these creatures to soar gently down to within a few inches of the coral. Soon, a dozen or more cleaner fish will swarm out of the coral to pick diligently at the mantas' bodies. The temptation to touch one should be overcome, for reaching out may frighten the animal away and destroy the enchanting moment. Often a manta ray will drift over your head so closely that it will have to raise its 'wings' to avoid touching you.

Opposite, above and below Manta rays (*Manta birostris*) gather at cleaning stations in channels where tidal waters flow in and out of the lagoon.

MELANESIA

Treasures Both Profuse and Rare

FIJI ISLANDS • SOLOMON ISLANDS

Melanesia, one of three recognized divisions of islands within the Pacific, includes the Fiji and Solomon islands which lie northeast of Australia in the southwestern part of the ocean. These island nations, together with Vanuatu and Papua New Guinea, are so close together on a map that one would expect their marine life to be identical. The good news for divers is that although the same species exist in all these areas, each location is worth exploring for its singular underwater topography and profusion of certain species.

Abel Tasman was given such an unfriendly reception when he chanced upon these magical islands that subsequent explorers avoided Fiji for 100 years. The Fijian archipelago consists of two major islands, Viti Levu and Vanua Levu, surrounded by several hundred smaller islands and reefs. As it lies along the Pacific's 'Ring of Fire' volcanic zone, divers may experience violent jolts from one of the underwater volcanoes in the area – a reminder of the planet's restless nature.

The Solomons seem almost quaint and unspoilt in comparison to Fiji's highly developed resort culture, which is characterized by family-oriented hotels offering popular watersports (in the Solomons, accommodation is often in the form of modest beachside bungalows or motels).

Fiji's well-known dive sites are all grouped in clusters, usually because they share undersea plateaus or atoll formations. The most publicized of these sites, including Beqa Lagoon (pronounced 'Benga') off the south coast of Viti Levu, Great Astrolabe Lagoon, and Rainbow Reef off the south coast of Vanua Levu, are all highly accessible from shore bases and as a result, Fiji has earned the undeserved reputation of being 'pretty, but tame'.

More recently, the rise of modern live-aboard diving in Fiji has opened up remote sites which are nothing short of sensational. Isolated locales such as E6 (well to the west of Rainbow Reef), Moturiki and Gau islands east of Viti Levu, and the Lau Islands which are situated even further east, are often swept by fierce currents which provide rich feeding and, consequently, vividly colourful soft corals. When the currents and the weather are right, Fiji offers sublime underwater photography.

Dive sites in the Solomons are so widely scattered that live-aboard diving is mandatory if you wish to see a representative selection of the best diving. There are land-based dive operations that provide access to fascinating wrecks as well as a few sensational reefs, but to dive varied sites, such as the Crack in the Island, Kicha, Mbula or Mary islands, only a live-aboard will do.

The Solomons are also home to sophisticated woodcarvers who produce sleek polished items in king and queen ebony wood. 'Spirit of Solomons' carvings feature intertwined marine creatures artfully executed in bas-relief. These and other pieces make memory-laden souvenirs for those fortunate enough to visit these myriad islands.

Opposite Divers prepare to descend to Tabua, a prime wall dive near Vanua Levu famous for its soft corals.
Top A glorious sunset over Munda Island in the Solomon Islands is a fitting end to a superb day's diving.

CLIMATE *Fiji* Jul–Aug cool to 21°C (70°F); Oct–Nov warm sultry weather until May. *Solomons* Tropical, warm and calm. Some rain Jan–Mar; 24–27°C (75–80°F).

BEST TIME TO GO Year-round for both; in *Fiji*, water colder and often clearer Jul–Aug.

GETTING THERE *Fiji* International flights from Australia, Tokyo and US to Nadi International Airport on Viti Levu. *Solomons* Flights from Fiji via Vanuatu, or from Auckland or Brisbane. Some resort islands require additional flights of an hour or more. Most operators provide transfers.

WATER TEMPERATURE *Fiji* Jul–Aug 23–24°C (74–76°F), Nov–May 27–28°C (81–83)°F. *Solomons* 26°C (79°F) in summer months, 29°C (84°F) Nov–Feb.

VISIBILITY *Fiji* Up to 38m (125ft) Jul–Aug, 21–30m (70–100ft) Nov–May. *Solomons* Commonly 23–30m (75–100ft); sometimes 38m (125ft) or better.

QUALITY OF MARINE LIFE *Fiji* Excellent; rich colours and great density. Live-aboards recommended for access to remote places. *Solomons* Good, but not as dense as Fiji; spectacular photographic subjects.

DEPTH OF DIVES All depths; most dives 21m (70ft) or less; some sheer walls justify 40m (130ft) (experienced divers only).

SNORKELLING Good on shallow reef tops.

DIVE PRACTICALITIES Level of experience required is site-specific; varies greatly.

FIJI ISLANDS

Diving in Fiji takes place mostly in currents. Many dives, however, are quite routine and well within the capabilities of certified divers. Occasionally, such as at Rainbow Reef or along the Great White Wall (one of the original sites that attracted divers to the Fiji Islands), the current actually affects the way one approaches the dive. When you hit the currents right in Fiji, you will be rewarded with extravagant photographic opportunities.

The Great White Wall

This exceptional dive site is situated along a particular stretch of outer fringing reef on the southern side of Vanua Levu, which drops off into the deep Somosomo Strait (also known as the Somosomo Channel) between the two main islands. The Great White Wall is the portion occurring between 27–73m (90–240ft). This vertical zone features endless colonies of a single species of ice-blue soft coral.

Currents in the Somosomo Strait can be strong, so diving here is only for those with a fair level of experience and competence. The best technique is to be completely prepared before you leave the boat. If you don't descend immediately to a depth of around 12m (40ft) on entering the water, you will be swept away by the current.

On the limestone substrate that forms the reef, every exposed structure touched by the current is carpeted with gaily coloured soft-coral colonies, crinoids, gorgonians, anemones, and other sea creatures. Countless tropical reef fish swirl and dance above the reef, feeding on passing plankton or on the profuse coral gardens themselves.

Above, left and right Fiji's strong, nutrient-rich currents yield jewel-bright soft coral gardens.

Right The venomous banded sea snake (*Laticauda colubrina*) swims to the surface to breathe air.

Small tunnels through the immense parapets of the reef lead to a sheer drop-off which plummets far below 91m (300ft), a considerable depth that is not for sport divers. Numerous other reefs in the Somosomo Strait are washed by the same nutrient-rich currents, but are dived less often. One such reef is E6, a sea mount which is best known for huge schools of pelagics (jacks, sharks, barracuda and turtles) that congregate around it.

Beqa Lagoon

The coral pinnacles of Beqa Lagoon are within easy reach of Pacific Harbour near Suva. The pinnacles rise from a huge submerged plateau

Above, left and right Feather stars on a gorgonian sea fan (*Subergorgia hicksoni*), and soft tree corals.

Right Filter-feeding Christmas-tree worms (*Spirobranchus giganteus*) embedded in stony coral.

between Beqa and Yanutha islands. The plateau is some 18–27m (60–90ft) below the surface, and some 50 or more sets of pinnacles are scattered across it for several miles. The tallest set, E.T. Pinnacles, and another known as Caesar's, rises from 27m (90ft) to within 3m (10ft) of the surface. Many of the pinnacles are fed by currents that flow across the plateau, and the sides that face the current are particularly stunning with a profusion of soft corals, crinoids and gorgonians on display.

Live-aboard boats have begun cruising further east in Fiji to a new selection of reefs. The pass at Wakaya has resident shoaling hammerheads, while Nigali Pass near Gau Island has grey reef and silvertip sharks, barracuda, and an overstuffed grouper; Moturiki is weather-exposed but offers colourful shallow pinnacles swarming with marine life; while further east, there is an action-packed channel and reef complex at the entrance to Falanghe, as well as a colossal chasm and arch formation a few miles to the southwest.

SOLOMON ISLANDS

Compared to the layered confusion and riot of life on Fiji's reefs, diving in the Solomons is quite different, with a stately wall of coral punctuated here and there by one or two precious gems. Perhaps this is as a result of slower currents, or maybe there are less structures directly facing the moving stream of food carried along by the currents. As a result, the Solomons' treasures are more obvious and less often hidden. You might see an anemone with a brilliant red mantle, a sassy white-bonnet clownfish, or a school of barracuda – none of these is a subtle attraction, rather an in-your-face extravagance.

Kicha and Mbulo islands

Both of these islands are situated at the southern end of Marovo Lagoon. Kicha is a well-endowed site with an amazing wall frequented by pelagics such as turtles and barracuda, as well as a buffalo-like herd of bumphead parrotfish. The vertical precipice is lined with fans and soft corals.

Opposite Barracuda (*Sphyraena* spp.) swim in tight formations for security.

Above Fusiliers (*Caesio* sp.) can be seen along the steep outer slopes of the reef.

Mbulo Island is one of the few places in the Solomons where you will find a density of marine life. At a zigzag corner, a steady current flows directly into a projecting wall that is 55m (180ft) wide. Here, 61m-tall (200ft) golden gorgonians march one after another into utter darkness; it is a moving sight and offers a cornucopia of photographic opportunities.

Mary Island

This prime site consists of a small coral structure nestled between the Russell Islands and Marovo Lagoon, and offers one of the best dives in the Solomons. A school of several hundred horse-eyed jacks ebbs and flows among the shallow ridges and valleys off the beach. If you swim upward off the outer reef slope into the blue water, a massive school of barracuda will sweep in and envelop you. Those dive sites which reliably deliver schooling pelagics are usually rated higher among divers than reefs filled with colour and small fish, and Mary Island is no exception.

Below Barracuda, horse-eyed jacks (*Caranx sexfasciatus*) and other fish move around in shoals, which confuses their predators and ensures that an individual is not singled out for attack.

CLIMATE Tropical and sultry; average temperatures 24–28°C (76–83°F). Cyclone season Jan–Mar; cool winters Jul–Aug.

BEST TIME TO GO Flat seas and cloudless skies in Oct–Nov. *Great Barrier Reef* has operators year-round; some operators offer trips to the *Coral Sea* May–Jan, although crossings can be rough.

GETTING THERE Regular flights to Cairns where boats are based for *Great Barrier Reef* sites. *Yongala* accessed from Townsville, Cod Hole from Port Douglas via Cairns. Live-aboard boats to *Coral Sea* depart from Townsville, Mackay, Cairns, Port Douglas.

WATER TEMPERATURE 24°C (75°F) Jul–Aug; 27°C (80°F) or more Nov–Mar.

VISIBILITY *Great Barrier Reef* Limited and dependent on tidal flows. Between 9–18m (30–60ft), especially in strong ebb tides. Where currents strong, advanced dive skills required. *Coral Sea* Among world's best, sometimes over 45m (150ft) in Oct–Nov.

QUALITY OF MARINE LIFE *Great Barrier Reef* Best in healthy coral areas or where fish are fed. *Coral Sea* Typified by large species, although not dense in marine life. Clear water yields strong colours.

DEPTH OF DIVES *Great Barrier Reef* On outer rim 6–18m (20–60ft). *Coral Sea* From near surface to 45m (150ft) or more.

SNORKELLING *Great Barrier Reef* Lucrative business. *Coral Sea* Excellent with clear water and reefs rising close to surface.

GREAT BARRIER REEF & CORAL SEA

Reefs Scattered Like Jewels in the Ocean

COD HOLE • *YONGALA* WRECK • PIXIE PINNACLE • DIAMOND REEF • LIHOU REEF

Stretching from Papua New Guinea in the north to Lady Elliott Island off Bundaberg in Queensland to the south, Australia's Great Barrier Reef is an astounding 2000km (1250 miles) or more long. It comprises some 2000 individual reefs and 71 coral islands, scattered like treasures off the Queensland coast and in the Coral Sea.

Queensland's most famous natural wonder is under the protection of the Great Barrier Reef Marine Park Authority, and is a listed World Heritage site. But the Great Barrier Reef and environs offer a wealth of diversions besides diving. Resort islands beckon with a wide range of watersports, and tropical forests such as Daintree National Park provide thrilling close encounters with crocodiles and hiking in the Mossman Gorge. Further north, the breathtaking, rugged coastal scenery of the Cape Tribulation National Park is not to be missed.

The Great Barrier Reef and Coral Sea were always among the earliest of the world's exotic diving destinations. In fact, the distant Coral Sea's crystal waters, with its atolls rising to the surface from extreme depths of some 1000m (3281ft) or more, surrounded by reefs such as Marion, Diamond and Lihou, were the ultimate target. However, a quick look at a map confirms that these sites require cruising of more than 322km (200 miles) out to sea; moreover, each one lies 160km (100 miles) or more beyond the outer perimeter of the Great Barrier Reef. These are significant distances to cover, even on a 10-day cruise, but when hardened and experienced divers see the constantly pristine condition of the Coral Sea sites after 20 years of occasional live-aboard visits, it is clear that the immense distances have protected these remote reefs from ruin. None could survive a daily assault of diver traffic.

The Coral Sea's waters tend to be gin-clear and the marine life is a rich tapestry of relatively few but large subjects. Everything seems to be oversized, from colossal coral colonies and big sharks to broad-backed rays. There may not be a profusion of creatures on any given atoll in the Coral Sea, but each specimen seems to be the biggest example you have ever seen.

The Great Barrier Reef, on the other hand, is an immense shallow, averaging 15–30m (50–100ft) deep and 80–160km (50–100 miles) wide. Vast tides – 3m (10ft) or more in some places – roar in and out of the reef passes each day. It is not surprising that fast currents of turbid lagoon-type water flow over the dive sites within the barrier reef, affecting visibility. In spite of this, a few dives of great impact can be enjoyed without travelling far beyond the Great Barrier Reef. Historically, live-aboard operators in the Coral Sea have woven the Barrier Reef's Cod Hole, Pixie Pinnacle and the *Yongala* Wreck into their itineraries.

Opposite Vast tidal flows of 3m (10ft) surge in and out of the lagoon between picturesque coral plateaus.
Top The Great Barrier Reef consists of countless reefs which nearly touch the ocean's limpid surface.

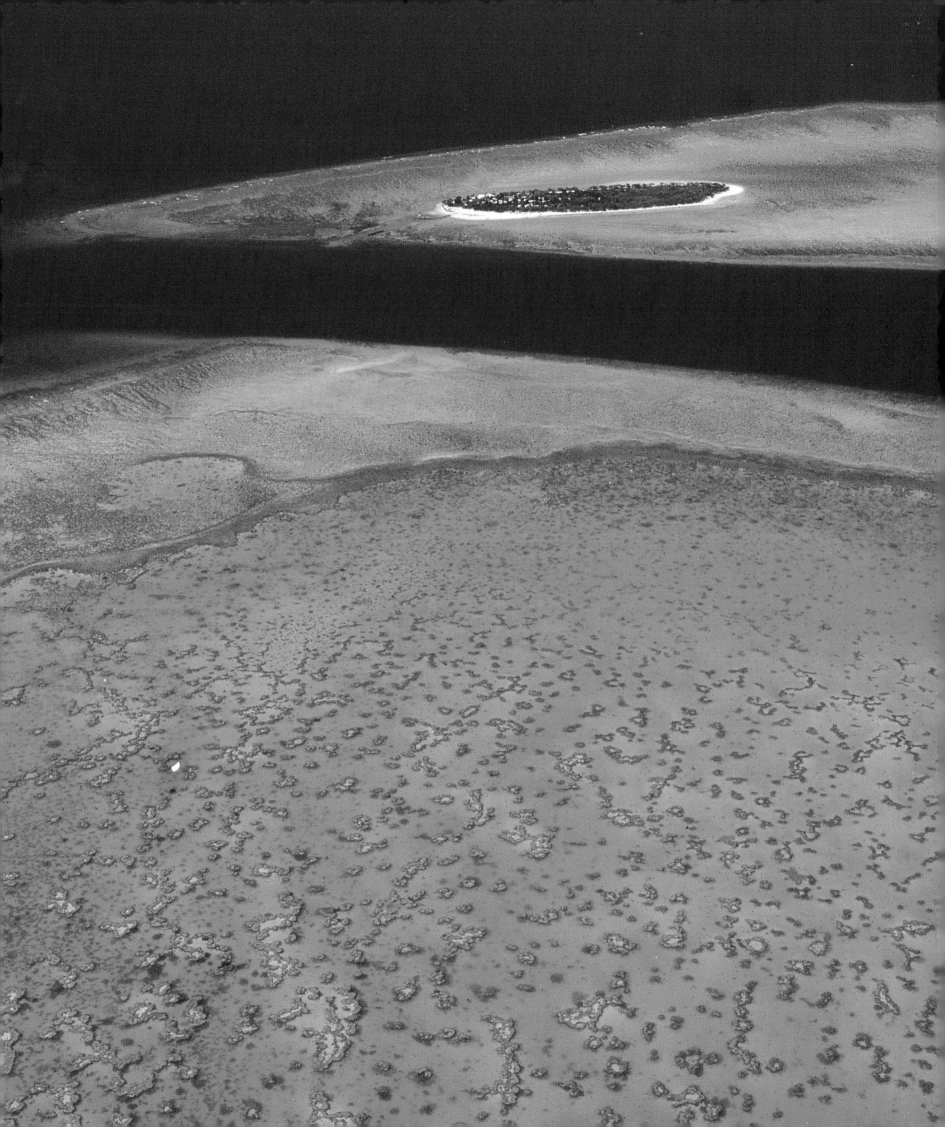

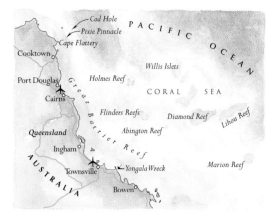

Above A lionfish (*Pterois volitans*) flares its lethal spines against the camouflage of a gorgonian sea fan.

Opposite Adult humphead, or Napoleon, wrasse (*Cheilinus undulatus*) are intelligent predators.

GREAT BARRIER REEF

Most scholars are taught that the Great Barrier Reef is the largest structure on earth; the real nature of the reef, though, is often left to one's imagination. Flying over it, a line of outer reefs is visible far out in the ocean. In the area eastward of Port Douglas, just north of Cairns, these outer flanks form a series of aquamarine lines lying end to end known as the Ribbon Reefs. Beyond these outer reefs the ocean plunges to extreme depths while inside, miles of sandy bottom are punctuated with a kaleidoscope of reef structures visible from the air. Further south, off Townsville and Rockhampton, there is a maze of reefs so complex that marine charts classify them as 'unexplored and hazardous'. In some sectors, eight-knot currents roar through the fiendishly complex passes when the tide comes in. The best dive sites are mainly found in the tidal passes closest to the open ocean.

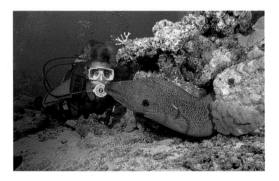

Cod Hole

Situated east-northeast of Lizard Island, the Cod Hole is a sheltered reef line where fishermen used to clean their catches and throw the offal over the side of the boat. A dozen years ago, a live-aboard skipper operating out of Cairns took divers to this spot and found plenty of fat, sassy potato cod groupers, huge Napoleon wrasse, pesky 1.8m-long (6ft) green moray eels, and other reef dwellers eager for handouts.

Today, despite the fact that the Cod Hole is an artificial feeding site, it is a trademark of Great Barrier Reef diving. Although some day boats from Lizard Island do make trips to the Cod Hole, it is essentially a live-aboard locale.

Yongala Wreck

The wreck of the *Yongala*, which lies some 322km (200 miles) further south within the Barrier Reef, is dense with coral growth and fish. Despite the characteristically turbid water, the spars are carpeted with soft corals, and the water is alive with schooling snappers, eagle rays, jacks, permits, spadefish, cobia, Napoleon wrasse, flowery cod, and barramundi cod. Here and there around the wreck you will encounter big stingrays, giant groupers, cat sharks, hawksbill turtles, sea snakes, and even an occasional guitar shark and cow-nosed ray. Although the *Yongala* wreck is richly endowed with marine life, the visibility is rarely more than 15m (50ft), and the location is completely exposed to rough weather and even the odd howling current.

Above The longnose hawkfish (*Oxycirrhites typus*) feeds among the branches of sea fans or soft corals.

Left The little spinecheek anemonefish (*Premnas biaculeatus*) has a horizontal spine on its gill plate.

Pixie Pinnacle

South of the Cod Hole, a 27m-tall (90ft) pinnacle of coral sits in the tidal flow of a long, meandering pass through the outer Barrier Reef. Known as Pixie Pinnacle, this live-aboard-only site was once blessed with profuse marine life: nudibranchs, clownfish, fairy basslets, rabbitfish, stonefish, and lionfish all thronged its tower. Many divers later, it exhibits signs of wear and tear but a nutrient-laden tidal flow still nourishes a riot of species.

Below left The Cod Hole is known for its massive moray eels which may approach you to be handfed.

Below A tiny bluestreaked cleaner wrasse (*Labroides dimidiatus*) swims alongside a massive potato cod grouper (*Epinephelus tukula*).

CORAL SEA

In 1972, the first boats made the crossing between the outer limits of the Great Barrier Reef and the mid-ocean atolls·of the Coral Sea in search of new diving horizons. It was soon apparent that the reefs of the southwestern area of the Pacific were too vast to appreciate in one trip. Those divers who were fortunate enough to share in the early adventures had several sources of anxiety. Few of them had ever been in the water with sea snakes, yet it was rumoured that Marion Reef was thick with them, and that the northern tip of this reef always attracted 30 or more sharks at a time. Needless to say, the pioneers of the Coral Sea all survived some spectacular shark feeds, so much so that divers now book exotic dive cruises precisely because they include one or more guaranteed shark encounters. The 'lethal' sea snakes were in fact everywhere on Marion Reef, but they were found to be lovable and curious, and made superb photographic subjects.

In the Coral Sea, you can dive with giant tuna, huge manta rays and monster nurse sharks while surrounded by immense soft-coral trees, all

Below Gorgonian sea fans (*Subergorgia mollis*) can reach a prodigious size in rich, feeding currents.

Below The distinct, massive hard coral (*Diploastrea heliopora*) has a long fossil history as a single species.

Below The giant clam (*Tridacna gigas*), often over 1m (40in) in length, lives on shallow reefs.

Above A female loggerhead turtle (*Caretta caretta*) struggles up a beach to deposit her eggs in the sand.

Opposite Slender anthias (*Luzonichthys waitei*) and longjawed, or sabre, squirrelfish (*Sargocentron spiniferum*) swim among soft corals and gorgonians.

in water with 60m (200ft) clarity or more. On one occasion, a diver came face to face with an enormous tiger shark, while in a separate incident, a huge hammerhead skidded to a stop right in front of a diver who had just completed a feeding session. Stories like these have spread the fame of the Coral Sea among divers throughout the world.

Today, remote oceanic atolls such as Marion, Diamond, Lihou and Abington remain unspoilt. Lihou has lots of sharks and Abington has a forest of 1.2m-tall (4ft) soft-coral trees in muted colours. There are other, newer sites with dramatic marine life, but these far-off reefs are still the standard by which all other challengers are tested.

Right A gorgonian sea fan (*Subergorgia mollis*) and soft tree corals grow at the entrance to a tunnel.

Below A large male loggerhead turtle follows his own sea route, undeterred by intruding humans.

NEW ZEALAND

Poor Knights Islands

TIE DYE ARCH • RIKORIKO CAVE

New Zealand has a reputation for offering adrenaline-charged outdoor activities, and its diving is no exception. With an intricate coastline equivalent in length to that of the continental United States of America, diving opportunities abound not only in New Zealand's Poor Knights Islands but also in the spectacular fjords of the country's southwest region.

Situated a mere 23km (14 miles) off the northeast coast of New Zealand's North Island, the uninhabited Poor Knights Islands offer unlimited world-class diving within a richly endowed reserve that is jealously protected. The main island group, which is some 5km (3 miles) long and 800m (half a mile) wide and consists of flat-topped, high-cliffed and densely forested volcanic rocks, is home to a prolific number of birds. Landing is forbidden except with prior permission and, as a result, the islands offer sanctuary to some fascinating creatures, including the tuatara – a lizard-like living fossil that only occurs on New Zealand's offshore islands – and some gigantic insects. The islands are also the only nesting ground on earth for a species of petrel that feeds in Antarctica. Between descents, divers can enjoy the songs of forest birds spilling from the tree-clad cliffs while being on the alert for the occasional free-falling tuatara.

The Poor Knights Islands were created some 10 million years ago when a volcano off North Island's east coast burst through the earth's crust in

a display of boiling molten rock. As the lava cooled, gas pockets, hot water and high-pressure steam sculpted the landscape into a maze of corridors, grottos and curved domes. Over time, with rising sea levels, the ocean eroded and carved the rock into a vast labyrinth of archways, tunnels and caverns. Here, the diving experience can be described as flying through the galleries in a giant's castle where the totally unexpected can happen, such as a thrilling encounter with a giant salp, a transparent open-ended floating barrel that is so big a diver can actually enter it and swim around inside.

Cave diving aside, the Poor Knights Islands are deservedly known as 'the islands of friendly fish'; the surrounding waters boast a wider range of fish species than the whole of New Zealand, and their size and approachability are a delight. A fusion of subtropical and temperate species includes coralfish, kelpfish, demoiselles, wrasse, scorpionfish, and moray eels.

Sea travel to the islands takes just over an hour from the marina at Tutukaka, which is a 30-minute drive from the inland city of Whangarei on North Island. Divers commute daily to the dive sites, although it is possible to arrange overnight trips for parties of up to eight. Tutukaka is the gateway to a wide variety of attractions along this stretch of coast, including New Zealand's top surfing spot, an array of tiny sheltered coves and isolated beaches, mangroves, and idyllic Matapouri Bay.

CLIMATE Warm and temperate; cool, wet and windy in winter (Jun–Oct). The islands are often very dry from Jan–Mar.

BEST TIME TO GO Year-round but warmer water Dec–May. In spring (Aug–Nov), water cool but ocean life rewarding, for example pearly nautilus and giant salp.

GETTING THERE Direct flights from major European cities, London, Singapore and US to Auckland; from here drive to Tutukaka, or fly to Whangarei. Most dive charters arrange transport from local airport. Dive boats make the 23km (14-mile) crossing to the islands in approximately one hour.

WATER TEMPERATURE Between 14–23°C (57–73°F); warmest Jan–May.

VISIBILITY 20–50m (60–150ft). Varies depending on plankton blooms (more intense and frequent in spring). Best Jan–Jul.

QUALITY OF MARINE LIFE Extremely diverse; many invertebrates, especially nudibranchs. Calm conditions on vertical walls make encrusting life very accessible. Reef fish abundant, large and friendly. Eagle and stingrays, moray eels and dolphins.

DEPTH OF DIVES 10–50m (30–150ft).

SNORKELLING Superb in Poor Knights; ride-on kayaks supplied by some charter boats especially for purpose of exploring.

DIVE PRACTICALITIES Dive certification required. Equipment hire available in Tutukaka. Most charter boats have guides.

Opposite A yacht sails past a sea arch carved from volcanic rock as it enters South Harbour off Aorangi.
Top The rugged islands form a marine reserve and landing is strictly forbidden without prior permission.

SEA CAVES

Scientists classify four basic types of sea caves, and the Poor Knights offer multiple examples of each. At water level there are caves and archways while below the water, blind alleys, or culs-de-sac, and tunnels await discovery (below). Each structure provides a unique combination of light penetration and water movement, factors which determine patterns of encrusting marine life and fish habitat. As such, sea caves provide a fascinating microcosm of the underwater environment.

Steady currents flowing through tunnels and archways transport an abundant supply of plankton in their stream, which provides a constant food source for fish and invertebrates. The walls are an Ali Baba's cave of encrusting treasures, and photographers can capture all the main groups of marine invertebrates within one frame in colours more intense than those found on a coral reef. In this environment of excess, it is possible to see the marine life that is usually found dispersed along a vast stretch of coast within a single dive.

By contrast, caves and culs-de-sac often present the same living conditions usually associated with extreme ocean depths, making them very appealing to snorkellers. Many inhabitants of sea caves require external energy in the form of light and movement to survive. In submerged caves below 30m (100ft), not much plankton penetrates beyond the portal, while in surface caves, wave action transports food right to the far recesses where strange deep-water sponges and solitary corals thrive in the darkness. In archways and submerged tunnels, water can flow all the way through, promoting growth of filter feeders.

Tie Dye Arch

At Pinnacle Rocks, south of Aorangi Island, there is a submerged throughway where conditions are near-perfect. Entering at twin Gothic Archways, the ocean courses steadily through a hallway six storeys high – a wet Westminster Abbey! Every inch of the vaulted ceilings, broad walls and massive boulders on the floor is encrusted with a crazy quilt of tiny mouths – a celebration of ocean life at its best. Fish often cram the hallway wall to wall and in summer, squadrons of stingrays cruise the portals.

Rikoriko Cave

A surface cul-de-sac, Rikoriko Cave is one of the largest sea caves in the world, a 200m (656ft) sphere half-filled with ocean; its tubular entrance is large enough to admit yachts! As you swim towards the back of Rikoriko at a depth of about 10m (33ft), the light level drops dramatically until it is equivalent to that at an ocean depth of 100m (328ft). Thus, in this sea cave, as your eyes adjust to the twilight, you find conditions applicable to the entire continental

shelf. In the furthest recesses, for example, lives a solitary lettuce-green coral polyp; previous records of its habitat were from sunless regions 2000m (6562ft) down. This is quite a dive!

Besides its wealth of sea caves and steep walls, the Poor Knights have much more to offer. Between the islands, sand-floored avenues and steep pinnacles provide optimal conditions for reef fish to flourish: a constant, gentle current from the tropics, shelter from wave violence, and sunlit seaweed jungles. Many divers prefer these forests with their fluctuant grace and colour to coral reefs.

Above A diver crouches on the sea bed as a short-tailed stingray (*Dasyatis brevicaudatus*) glides peacefully overhead.

Centre The Nembrotha nudibranch (*Nembrotha* spp.) is dressed in striking colours that are distasteful to its predators.

Opposite Many species of fish are attracted to feed on plankton which have been disturbed by a diver.

Map labels:
Wild Beast Point
Northern Arch
Tawhiti Rahi Island
Cleanerfish Bay
Middle Arch
POOR KNIGHTS ISLANDS (New Zealand)
Serpent Rock
Nursery Cove
Rikoriko Cave
Aorangi Island
Oculina Point
Blue Maomao Arch
South Harbour
Pinnacle Rocks & Tie Dye Arch
(± 4.8 km / 3 miles)

GALÁPAGOS, COCOS & MALPELO ISLANDS

Vast Schools of Hammerheads

GOLDEN TRIANGLE

CLIMATE *Galápagos* Dry and warm in spring and autumn; summers windy with rough water for ocean cruises. *Cocos* and *Malpelo* Tropical; strong winds in summer and autumn can affect crossings.

BEST TIME TO GO *Galápagos* Clearest water from Oct–Nov; spring months for nesting birds and fascinating land walks. *Cocos* Year-round destination; *Malpelo* Dec–Jul.

GETTING THERE *Galápagos* Boats depart from San Cristobal or from Baltra Island, via a connecting flight from Quito. *Cocos* and *Malpelo* Fly to San Jose, Costa Rica. Boat departs from Puntarenato for Cocos, or take an early morning flight to Golfito where live-aboard cruises leave for Malpelo.

WATER TEMPERATURE Variable, between 18–24°C (65–75°F). *Galápagos* Full wetsuit with hood recommended. *Cocos* and *Malpelo* 27°C (80°F); sharp thermoclines from 9–30m (30–100ft).

VISIBILITY *Galápagos* Averages 9–21m (30–70ft); *Cocos* and *Malpelo* 9–24m (30–80ft), occasionally 24–30m (80–100ft).

QUALITY OF MARINE LIFE Superb and varied; northern Galápagos islands for hammerheads. *Cocos* and *Malpelo* have jacks, goatfish and soldierfish in excess.

DEPTH OF DIVES *Galápagos* 5–24m (15–80ft); *Cocos* and *Malpelo* Surface to 37m (120ft); depends on location of sharks.

DIVE PRACTICALITIES Not for novices; comprehensive travel insurance advised.

Together with the far-flung Cocos and Malpelo islands, the Galápagos Islands form a roughly triangular configuration in the eastern Pacific that is sometimes referred to as the Golden Triangle. A rare breed of diver is lured to these isolated outposts where vast squadrons of hammerheads make their way back and forth across the ocean, navigating by means of the earth's magnetic field in a series of repetitive seasonal and daily migrations; to witness this cosmic ballet of sinister shapes is quite an experience.

Originally named Encantadas, which means 'enchanted', by the Spanish, the Galápagos Islands are situated on the equator about 966km (600 miles) west of Ecuador off South America. Swept by convoluted, often treacherous currents, this group of remote oceanic islands is renowned for its strange and often inexplicable natural history. It was here that Charles Darwin's leaps of intellectual analysis led to the development of the theory of the origin of species. The Galápagos Islands are also famous for their giant tortoises, which can be viewed in captivity at the Charles Darwin Research Station on Santa Cruz. Since the equally remote Seychelles archipelago is the only other place on earth where giant tortoises are found, it is no wonder that the sparsely vegetated volcanic landscapes of the Galápagos have earned their appellation as 'the enchanted islands'.

These islands are large and widely dispersed, and are only accessible by boat; crossings between the islands can take from two to 14 hours. Specialized live-aboard expeditions to the Galápagos group began in 1972 when the first organized diving party visited this region. The 966km (600-mile) flight from Guayaquil on the coast of Ecuador across open ocean to Baltra Island, which lies just west of Santa Cruz, does not prepare one for the sight of the island's dramatic spires of laval rock thrusting out of the featureless sea. Boobies, frigate birds, the waved albatross, and other sea birds swoop and wheel in the sky, eagerly scanning the waters for their prey.

The succession of endemic or unusual creatures above and below the water is overwhelming. The islands abound with the unexpected, and each seems to hold its own surprise, from fur sea lions and penguins to marine iguanas that slither into the water at low tide to munch on seaweed.

Scattered trees, cacti and briar bushes contrast with white sand beaches and lush vegetation; the only constant is the sun-baked rock. Underwater, oceanic currents come together and snake their way between the parapets of unyielding volcanic stone. The result is a broth of cool nutrient-laden water that yields a dense marine biomass. Huge schools of horse-eyed jacks, goatfish, creolefish and other species swarm everywhere.

Opposite Bartolome Island's Pinnacle Rock is typical of the stark volcanic outcrops that make up Galápagos.
Top Malpelo Island's granite cliffs are in direct contrast to the riches found below the surface of the water.

Above Few experiences are as initially chilling as one's first sight of schooling hammerhead sharks.

Left and below Most of the hammerheads seen by divers are females; they are all nearsighted.

Galápagos Islands

Considering the immense distances that have to be covered and the extraordinary quality of the marine environment, it is well worth spending at least 10 to 14 days diving and exploring these fascinating islands. Land walks, which are usually included in live-aboard-cruise itineraries, are strictly controlled in the interests of minimizing human impact. Approximately one-third of all inshore marine species in the Galápagos are unique to the islands, including many-armed *Heliaster* starfish, horned moray eels with yellow eyes and the wrasse-assed bass. Mostly, though, they are Galápagos sub-species of fish found off Panama, Baja and Chile. Besides the schooling hammerheads, which are most prolific around the far northern islands of Wolf and Darwin, there are also giant loggerhead turtles, sperm whales,

ocean sunfish, and Galápagos sharks. Volcanic granite and basalt rocks, ranging in colour from tan to black, are pockmarked with burrowing sea urchins and vertical walls bloom with lush trees of black coral whose polyps form an eerie golden yellow glow in the deep gloom.

Cocos Island

For many years sporadic reports from yachting nomads made mention of a forbidding fortress some 483km (300 miles) north of the northern Galápagos islands, Wolf and Darwin off the Columbian coast, whose waters teemed with hammerhead sharks and other pelagics. When modern live-aboard vessels finally began offering cruises to Cocos Island with its strange rubble beaches, beautiful waterfalls and jungle-clad cliffs, the flood of people clamouring to dive with sharks confirmed a major new trend in the sport.

Cocos Island's main 21km² (13-sq-mile) mass is surrounded by huge spikes of volcanic rock, known as outrider spires, up to 0.5km (a quarter mile) offshore. Shoaling hammerheads regularly swarm around certain of these islets. One spot in particular is known as Dirty Rocks, and is perhaps the most reliable hammerhead site on the planet. The number of sharks may vary from a couple of hundred to a thousand or more, sending divers' pulse rates soaring. These rocks are washed by modest currents that can transport divers a further 0.5km (a quarter mile) or more in the course of a dive. The currents provide free transportation, allowing you to drift through colossal aggregations of horse-eyed jacks, creolefish, soldierfish, goatfish, and other species; in fact, any kind of fish you see is likely to be in schools of thousands. Encounters with whale sharks, humpback whales, sailfish, giant manta rays, wahoo, and other large pelagic species are also guaranteed.

Malpelo Island

In physical terms, Malpelo, an island which lies some 500km (310 miles) off the western coast of Colombia, is a miniature of Cocos Island. It comprises a central massif of grey granite which soars vertically out of the sea with sheer walls that extend in places to 152m (500ft). A few young Colombian soldiers live high up on the main island, contributing the only touch of humanity to the unforgiving moonscape. North and south of the island, outrider spires, reminiscent of Cocos, are scattered at the edges of the landmass. Schooling hammerheads are found close to the

surface all around the main and satellite islands, and in addition some sites off the main island boast huge shoals of goatfish, creolefish, groupers, whitestriped angelfish, fearless pesky amberjacks and green moray eels.

Malpelo is a fairly recent diving discovery and its marine life is relatively unaffected as a result. Here, the hammerhead sharks are so shy that they respond to diver intrusion by spiralling slowly downwards to the safety of deeper, darker water. At a depth of 30m (100ft), divers are motioned to sit quietly on the rocks, minimize their breathing, and wait for the sharks to move closer.

Left At low tide, marine iguanas (*Amblyrhynchus cristatus*) in their hundreds enter the water around the Galápagos Islands to feed on shallow algae.

Right Galápagos sea lions (*Zalophus californianus galapagensis*) are extremely playful underwater. They enjoy showing off in front of divers, and twist and turn in endless graceful configurations.

CALIFORNIA

Catalina Island

CASINO POINT UNDERWATER PARK • FARNSWORTH BANKS

Catalina, or Santa Catalina as it is also known, is a small island approximately 32km (20 miles) long and 13km (8 miles) across at Long Point, its widest point. It narrows further to 800m (half a mile) at the isthmus between two harbours in the northwest part of the island. With its easily accessible sandy beaches, rugged scenery, unusual plants, and fascinating array of wildlife (deer, buffalo and island fox), it is difficult to imagine that this wonderfully laid-back US territory lies less than 48km (30 miles) from the urban sprawl of Los Angeles on the Californian mainland. Over the years, Catalina Island has been a haven for sun-worshipping Indians, ranchers and smugglers. William Wrigley Jr., heir to the Wrigley chewing gum dynasty, bought controlling interest in the Santa Catalina Island Company in 1919 and started transforming the island into a prime holiday destination. Present ownership of the company still stems from Wrigley's original stock purchases.

As a result of the cool, clear seas off California, the underwater world is dominated by kelp, particularly forests of giant kelp and their rich associated fauna. Although there are dense kelp forests along much of the Californian coastline, Catalina offers particularly easy and enjoyable access to a variety of sites within a defined area.

The Santa Catalina Island Conservancy, a nonprofit foundation, acquired title to 16,997ha (42,000 acres), or 86 per cent, of Catalina in 1974 in order to ensure its conservation as wilderness. Today, 90 per cent of the island is wilderness, which means that according to statutory law it has to remain in a natural state in perpetuity. Visitors should take time to explore Catalina's wild but beautiful interior. As it is not possible to hire a car, options include taking a bus tour, hiking one of the well-marked trails, cycling, or horse riding.

Access to Catalina is via a regular ferry service which runs between the island's only city, Avalon, and the Californian mainland. Home to fewer than 3000 permanent residents, Avalon offers a wide variety of hotel accommodation and is very much a family-oriented resort. A good range of hotels offers watersports and island excursions, as well as numerous shops and restaurants; the city even boasts a vibrant nightlife. A few easily accessible sandy beaches near the centre of Avalon are worth visiting. Accommodation is best booked in advance, particularly if your stay includes a weekend in the busy summer or autumn months.

Avalon has at least two well-stocked dive shops, and several charter boats from which to choose. Shore diving is, however, excellent and several sites can be reached by taxi or on foot; hand carts to transport your equipment are also available for hire from the dive shops. Besides diving, Catalina is famous for its spectacular fishing grounds, and is also a popular stop-off point for motorized cruisers and yachts.

Opposite Casino Point, site of Catalina's only casino and museum, is also the entry point for shore dives.

Top The calm waters below Casino Point are conducive to safe exits once a dive has been completed.

CLIMATE More temperate than southern Californian coast, which has mild winters and warm summers. Temperatures rarely rise above 25°C (77°F) in summer, seldom drop below 10°C (50°F) in winter.

BEST TIME TO GO Autumn (Sep–Nov) is best; water calmest, clearest and warmest.

GETTING THERE Direct flights to Los Angeles in California from virtually anywhere, followed by one- or two-hour ferry journey from the large terminals at Long Beach or San Pedro.

WATER TEMPERATURE Approximately 20°C (68°F) in summer and autumn; full wetsuit with hood recommended.

VISIBILITY Usually 10–30m (30–100ft).

QUALITY OF MARINE LIFE Excellent giant kelp forests. Wide variety of solitary and shoaling fish, including barracuda; also crayfish, nudibranchs, starfish and soft corals. Larger animals include bat rays, seals and sea lions.

DEPTH OF DIVES Sites range from 10–30m (30–100ft).

SNORKELLING Excellent shore-based snorkelling from Casino Point and Lovers' Cove (only snorkelling permitted at latter).

DIVE PRACTICALITIES Recognized dive certification required for any equipment hire or boat diving. All gear available for hire, including trolleys for easy shore diving. Training is available.

FORESTS OF GIANT KELP

The giant kelp forests off Catalina Island require ample sunlight and cool, nutrient-rich waters in order to flourish. A mature forest is not, as some may imagine, an impenetrable tangle of seaweed but an arena of quite breathtaking beauty that is home to a wonderful array of marine life. Individual plants can reach up to the surface from depths of 30m (100ft), but are widely spaced so that there is plenty of room to swim between them. Sunlight can penetrate easily and the scenes created by shafts of light reflecting off silvery shoaling fish are often remarkable. The experience of swimming through a kelp forest can really only be compared to the imaginary pleasure of flying through a tropical rainforest, with fish replacing exotic birds for company.

While the sandy bottom of the kelp forest is always fascinating to explore, the shallower upper reaches of the canopy are also worthwhile for their different species of fish.

Casino Point Underwater Park

The prime shore-diving spot is the underwater park at Casino Point, a landmark situated a few minutes' walk from the centre of Avalon. The park was established in 1962 by the then owners of Catalina Divers' Supply, a dive shop in Avalon. Buoys at the surface keep out any boat traffic, and the underwater landscapes are totally unspoilt.

The sea bed slopes steeply out from the shore to 30m (100ft) at the outer edge of the park. Kelp growth is prolific and the marine life spectacular, with a variety of invertebrates and fish species. Brilliant-orange Garibaldi damselfish, kelp bass, sheephead wrasse, señoritas, rock wrasse, and numerous species of shoaling fish are all common to the park, while large bat rays are often sighted. Invertebrates include crabs, spiny lobsters, starfish and some exquisitely coloured nudibranchs. Other shore dives are possible at Ring Rock and on the sea-fan-covered wreck of the *Valiant*, which lies in about 30m (100ft) of water.

Farnsworth Banks

Boat dives are possible at sites such as Hen Rock, Pirate's Cove, Seal Rock, and the Italian Gardens, which have caves, gullies, kelp forests, sandy areas, as well as plentiful marine life, including moray eels, octopus, mantis shrimps, and bat rays. Sea lions can also be seen cavorting around Seal Rock. All these sites lie within easy reach of Avalon. However, it is the Farnsworth Banks on the Pacific side of the island attract attract divers from all over North America. Unfortunately, this site can only be dived in very favourable conditions. Spectacular rock pinnacles and drop-offs support dense growths of the rare purple California hydrocoral and are home to various rays and shoaling fish, including barracuda.

Below The ugly, inquisitive kelp bass (*Paralabrax clathratus*) exhibits no fear when divers are nearby.

Left, from top to bottom Kelp diving has been described as flying through a tropical rainforest.

Above Striking Garibaldi damselfish (*Hypsypops rubicundus*) – a juvenile (top) and adult (bottom).

Opposite Giant kelp forests form a nursery and a safe habitat for countless marine species.

Following pages These matching spiny lobsters (*Panulirus interruptus*) might have been a cinch to capture on film, but they retain an elusive air.

ACKNOWLEDGMENTS

Text contributors: **Guy Buckles** *Israel, Egypt, Sudan, Indonesia* **Wade Doak** *New Zealand* **Nick Hanna** *Thailand* **Jack Jackson** *General Introduction, Cuba, Bahamas, Dutch Antilles, Malaysia, Philippines* **Stefania Lamberti** *South Africa, Maldives* **Fred Dembny** *Puerto Rico* **Jürgen Warnecke** *Canary Islands* **Friedrich Naglschmid** *Sardinia* **Paul Naylor** *California* **Text adapted by Jane Maliepaard** *Maldives, Papua New Guinea, Micronesia, Melanesia, Great Barrier Reef & Coral Sea, Galápagos, Cocos & Malpelo Islands* **Lawson Wood** *Mexico, Cayman Islands, Scotland, South Africa, Seychelles*

The publishers would like to thank Jack Jackson for his invaluable assistance throughout the project, during which he gave generously of his time, energy and immense knowledge.

Particular thanks to the photographers Patrick Wagner, Danja Köhler and Peter Pinnock for all their additional help with picture selection and identification, and diving tales… Thanks also to Ann Baggaley for her eleventh-hour editorial input.

Copyright © in photographs rests with the following photographers and/or their agents: **Kelvin Aitken** *pp. 58, 101 (top & bottom), 150 (top & bottom left), 151 (left: top & bottom, & right), 158 (top left & bottom), 159 (left, & right: top, 2nd from top, 2nd from bottom & bottom);* **Franco Banfi** *pp. 48–49, 52, 53, 54 (left & top right), 55;* **Ashley Boyd** *pp. 105, 106 (2nd from top & bottom), 107 (top left), 108 (bottom), 109 (top), 117 (bottom left), back cover (top left);* **Gerald Cubitt** *pp. 118, 119;* **Kevin Deacon (Ocean Earth Images)** *pp. 11 (right), 98, 146, 148, 149 (top: left & right, & centre & bottom right), 150 (bottom: centre & right);* **Roger de la Harpe (Natal Parks Board)** *p. 78;* **Fred Dembny** *pp. 30, 31, 32 (left & right), 33 (top & bottom);* **Roger Grace** *endpapers (3rd from right), pp. 152, 153, 154 (top, centre & bottom), 155;* **Jack Jackson** *pp. 11 (2nd from right), 22, 23, 24 (right: top, centre & bottom), 25 (top left), 59, 60, 61 (bottom: left, centre & right), 70, 71, 72, 73, 74 (top & bottom), 75, 110, 112 (right), 114, 115, 116 (bottom: left, 2nd from left, 2nd from right & right), 117 (top left & right);* **Les Kemp** *pp. 34, 35, 37 (left & right), back cover (bottom right);* **Danja Köhler** *pp. 6, 7 (top, centre & bottom), 10 (left), 11 (left), 27, 28 (left), 93 (bottom left & right), 113 (right top), 116 (top), 122–123, 124, 125, 126 (top, & bottom: left & right), 127 (top, & bottom: left, centre & right), 128, 129 (left: top & bottom, & right), 130 (top: left, centre & right, & bottom: left, centre & right), 131, 134, 135 (left), 136 (left, & right: top & bottom), 138 (top: left & right, & bottom), 139, back cover (top centre, centre left & centre right);* **Stefania Lamberti** *pp. 11 (2nd from left), 83 (top right), 91;* **Paul Naylor** *pp. 160, 161, 162 (left: top, centre & bottom, & right: top, centre & bottom), 163, 164–165, back cover (top right);* **Photo Access (Philip Barker)** *p. 26;* **Photo Access (Doug Perrine)** *p. 36 (right);* **Photo Access (Patrick Wagner)** *pp. 62, 79, 84, 85, 86, 87, 88 (top);* **Photo Index (Richard Woldendorp)** *p. 97;* **Peter Pinnock** *front cover, spine, endpapers (left), pp. 2, 4, 5, 61 (top), 66 (top), 80 (top: left, 2nd from left, 2nd from right, right, & bottom: left & right), 81 (top left), 82, 83 (top left, & bottom: left, centre & right), 144, 145 (top, & bottom: left, centre & right);* **Linda Pitkin** *pp. 69 (right: top & bottom), 76–77, 112 (left), 113 (right: 2nd from top), back cover (bottom left);* **Planet Earth Pictures (Kurt Amsler)** *p. 24 (left), 54 (bottom right);* **Planet Earth Pictures (Chris Huxley)** *p. 36 (left);* **Planet Earth Pictures (John Lythgoe)** *pp. 50, 51;* **Planet Earth Pictures (Jeannie Mackinnon)** *p. 137 (top);* **Planet Earth Pictures (Pete Oxford)** *p. 157;* **Planet Earth Pictures (Doug Perrine)** *pp. 25 (top right), 28 (right);* **Planet Earth Pictures (Linda Pitkin)** *p. 25 (bottom), 38–39;* **Planet Earth Pictures (Carl Roessler)** *p. 137 (bottom);* **Planet Earth Pictures (Marty Snyderman)** *p. 158 (top right);* **Planet Earth Pictures (Darryl Torckler)** *p. 29;* **Carl Roessler** *pp. 96, 99, 132, 133, 135 (right), 156;* **Rebecca Saunders** *pp. 113 (right: 2nd from bottom & bottom), 120, 121 (left, & right: top, 2nd from top, centre, 2nd from bottom, bottom), 147, 149 (bottom left);* **Geoff Spiby** *endpapers (2nd & 3rd from left, & right), pp. 1, 3, 56–57, 64 (top & bottom), 65, 66 (bottom), 67 (top: left, centre & right, & bottom), 68 (left, & right: top & bottom), 69 (left: top & bottom), 93 (top left), 168;* **Mark Strickland (Oceanic Impressions)** *pp. 10 (right), 100, 102–103, 104, 106 (top & 2nd from bottom), 107 (bottom left & right), 108 (top), 109 (bottom);* **Patrick Wagner** *pp. 90, 92 (left & right), 94, 95, 140, 141, 142 (top: left & right, & bottom), 143 (top: left & right, & bottom);* **Jürgen Warneke** *pp. 44, 45, 46, 47;* **Lawson Wood** *endpapers (2nd from right), pp. 10 (2nd from left & 2nd from right), 12–13, 14, 15, 16 (top & bottom), 17 (top, & bottom: left, centre & right), 18, 19, 20 (left & right), 21 (left, centre & right), 40, 41, 42 (top: left & right, & bottom: left & right), 43, 63, 64 (left), 81 (top right & bottom), 88 (bottom), 89 (left & right), 111, 113 (left), 166–167, back cover (centre middle & bottom centre).*